Island Home

ISLAND HOME
The Blasket Heritage

GEORGE THOMSON

and

GEORGE THOMSON
a memoir

by
TIM ENRIGHT

BRANDON

23979

Published in 1988 by
Brandon Book Publishers Ltd
Dingle, Co. Kerry, Ireland
and 27 South Main Street
Wolfeboro, New Hampshire 03894-2069, USA

British Library Cataloguing in Publication Data
Thomson, George, 1903-1987
    Island home.
    1. Writers. (County) writers. Great
    Blasket island writers. Critical
    studies
    I. Title
    809'.89419'6

    ISBN 0-86322-101-7

This book is published with the financial assistance of
The Arts Council/An Chomhairle Ealaíon, Ireland

Cover design: Paula Nolan
Typesetting: Koinonia
Printed by Billings Ltd, Worcester

Contents

List of Illustrations

Photographs taken by George Thomson on the Blaskets, 1923–34

The Blasket Books

Tomás Ó Criomhthain (Tomás O'Crohan)
Réiltíní Óir
Allagar na hInise   *Island Cross-Talk*
An tOileánach   *The Islandman*
Dinnsheanchas na mBlascaodaí
Seanchas ón Oileán Tiar

Muiris Ó Súilleabháin (Muiris O'Sullivan)
Fiche Blian ag Fás   *Twenty Years A-Growing*

Peig Sayers
Peig   *Peig*
Machnamh Seanmhná   *An Old Woman's Reflections*
Scéalta ón mBlascaod

Seán Ó Criomhthain (Seán O'Crohan)
Lá Dár Saol
Leoithne Aniar

Mícheál Ó Gaoithín (Mícheál O'Guiheen)
Is Truagh ná Fanann an Óige   *A Pity Youth Does Not Last*
Coinnle Corra
Beatha Pheig Sayers

Máire Ní Ghuithín (Máire Guiheen)
An tOileán a Bhí
Bean an Oileáin

Eibhlís Ní Shúilleabháin (Eibhlís O'Sullivan)
Letters from the Great Blasket

Seán Sheáin Í Cearnaigh (Seán O'Kearney)
An tOileán a Tréigeadh
Iarbhlascaodach ina Dheoraí

Note of thanks

In his Memoir of my late husband, Tim Enright relates how the Reverend Professor Pádraig Ó Fiannachta collaborated with George in translating St Augustine's *Confessions* into Irish. He describes how Pádraig also published a second edition of the Gaelic text of *Twenty Years A-Growing* and translations from Greek into Irish found after George's death. I wish now to thank him for agreeing, with his usual generosity, to the publication of this amended and enlarged edition of *The Blasket that was*, originally published by him at Maynooth.

I would like to thank Anne Baird of Birmingham for her expert handling of George's photographs, some of which were taken as far back as 1923. She also photographed Muiris O'Sullivan's drawings, made to go with his manuscript of *Twenty Years A-Growing*.

I also wish to thank my daughter, Margaret Alexiou, who helped to revise this book and took down "The Sorrowful Cliff" from her father's dictation.

I am grateful to friends and Blasket-lovers for their help and encouragement, especially Seán Ó Lúing, Ray Stagles and Muiris Mac Conghail. Above all my thanks are due to Tim Enright for contributing the Memoir and for his unfailing support and expert advice, both during George's lifetime and since his death, in preparing the book for publication.

Katharine Thomson
Birmingham, March 1988

Island Home

The Blasket Heritage

Preface

The Great Blasket is the largest of a group of small islands lying off the south-west coast of Ireland. It is now deserted, but was inhabited till recently by a small Gaelic-speaking fishing community. There was no shop, no tavern, no post-office, no policeman, no doctor, no priest. It was often cut off from the mainland for weeks on end by bad weather.

Communities of this type, based on kinship and co-operation, are still to be found in many parts of the world, though they are rapidly disappearing. But in one respect the Blasket was unique. During the past half-century natives of this village have produced more than a dozen books. Several of them have been translated into English and one of them – *Twenty Years A-Growing* – has become world-famous. Taken together, they give us a comprehensive and intimate picture of the life of such a community, written by the Islanders themselves. In the following pages an attempt is made to explain how these seemingly backward Islanders came to make so distinguished a contribution to contemporary literature.

For the sake of uniformity in the rendering of Gaelic names and idioms, all passages quoted from the books are given in my own translation. In dealing with personal names I have (with certain exceptions) followed the common practice of combining the Gaelic form of the first name with the anglicised form of the surname.

My thanks are due to Mr T. Enright, without whose help and encouragement this book could not have been written.

George Thomson
Birmingham, 1987

Before the Famine

It is uncertain how far back in history the Blasket Islands had been inhabited. Written records are few, but local traditions throw some light on the question.

The earliest of these dates from the defeat of the Spanish Armada. In September 1588 one of the ships, *Santa Maria de la Rosa*, was wrecked off Dunmore Head. This event was remembered both in Dunquin, on the opposite mainland, and in the Island itself. Seán O'Crohan recalls how in his childhood, when walking through the village after dark, the children used to scare one another by saying, "The old Spanish woman will come before us tonight". It was only later that he learned who this Spanish woman was:

> It seems that, after the ship went down, a woman's body was cast up on the strand of the Island. According to the old tales she was a rich lady, adorned with gold rings and bracelets, and she was buried at Castle Point, where the graveyard is today. The strange thing is, she was not buried in the graveyard itself, but just outside it. An old man pointed it out to me many years ago.
>
> *Lá Dár Saol*

In the year 1641 Pierce Ferriter led a rebellion against the English. He was defeated and took refuge in the Great Blasket,

13

where he had a small castle. The Islanders hid him from his pursuers in a cave, still known as Pierce's Cave, where he composed this quatrain:

> O God above, do you pity me as I am,
> A homeless wretch, who scarcely sees the day,
> The drip from the slab overhead falling into my ear,
> And the drone of the sea at my heels?

The Ferriters were a family of Anglo-Norman origin who had been settled in this part of Kerry since the thirteenth century and had become completely gaelicised – "more Irish than the Irish themselves". They had a castle in Ballyferriter and possessed many estates in the district, including the Blasket Islands. Pierce was head of the family. He was a cultured man and a poet of distinction. We do not know what services he claimed from his retainers, but he seems to have been more of a clan chief than a feudal lord. The Blasket people had many stories about him which show that they regarded him as one of themselves. He was "their winning card, their guardian hound".[1] In 1653 he was captured and executed and his estates were confiscated. The Islanders then became rent-paying tenants subject to English landowners.

The rent was payable in money, so they sold their surplus of fish and livestock at the local market in Dingle and at the same time they bought there such necessities as they could not produce for themselves. In this way they became accustomed to the use of money as a medium of exchange and to regular production for the market. The rent was heavy. They had no security of tenure and no incentive to improve their holdings. These conditions prevailed throughout rural Ireland, except where the land had been occupied by settlers from Britain. But the Blasket people possessed one advantage. They were protected to some extent by the sea. It often happened that a raiding party of bailiffs and police would be prevented from landing by volleys of stones from the cliff-top.

Throughout the eighteenth century the history of the Blasket Islands is a blank, except for one writer's report that in the year 1756 there were five or six families living there. That would be forty to fifty persons. So small a community could have survived without undue pressure on the soil. But these conditions did not last. During the century 1750-1850 there was a steady drift of dispossessed peasant families from the interior of the country to the barren mountains of the western seaboard. The movement had begun with the first English plantations in the sixteenth century; now it gathered pace and culminated in the Great Famine of 1846-47. The evicted families were attracted to the Blasket by the abundance of wild life – rabbits, sea-birds and shellfish. Even the outlying islands were occupied. It was during these years that the Sullivans, Carneys and Donlevys settled in the main island. Muiris O'Sullivan could point to the plot of land in Ventry from which his great-grandfather had been evicted and could name the agent who evicted him. The resulting congestion was a major factor in aggravating the effects of the Famine. The situation in the Blaskets was relieved to some extent in 1850 when a ship carrying wheat was wrecked off the Islands. Even so, the population was reduced from 153 persons (28 families) in 1841 to 97 persons (19 families) in 1851.[2]

The Famine and after

The Great Famine of 1846-47 was not caused by a shortage of food but by a failure of the potato crop due to bad weather. While the peasantry starved, vast quantities of grain were shipped across to England, where imports from Ireland were protected under the Corn Laws. Agricultural prices rose continuously, but this brought no benefit to the producers because the landlords used it as a pretext to raise the rent. Since most of the big landlords were absentees living in London, the wealth created in Ireland was transferred to England where it augmented the capital available for industrial development.

The effect of these conditions on the mass of smallholders was to confine them to a potato diet. Potatoes are cheaper to produce than cereals because they require a smaller acreage to yield a given amount of food value. The failure of the potato crop was general throughout Europe, but only in Ireland had the peasantry been reduced to dependency on it. The Famine was aggravated by cholera and typhus: within ten years the rural population was almost halved. The population of the country as a whole fell from over eight million in 1841 to less than five million in 1891, and this at a time when the population of England was increasing more rapidly than ever before.

The living conditions of the Blasket Islanders in the post-Famine period may be judged from what Tomás O'Crohan tells us of their housing:

> As for the houses we had in my youth, and for some time
> after, they varied, just as they do in other places. Some of
> them were quite elegant, others very wretched. Some were
> no more than ten feet by eight, others up to fifteen or twenty
> feet in length. The house was divided into two parts by a
> dresser standing out from the wall as far as the middle of
> the floor, where it was met by a partition extended from
> the other wall. On the far side were two beds, with people
> in them, two pigs under one bed and potatoes under the
> other. Between the beds a big chest lay up against the gable
> wall. On the near side, the kitchen side, the family, perhaps
> ten of them, used to spend the day, or part of it. Up against
> the partition there might be a hen coop and beside it a
> broody hen in an old cooking-pot. At night there would be
> a cow or two or a couple of calves, an ass, two dogs tied to
> the wall or let loose about the house. If the family was a
> large one, there would be two post-beds in the corner, or
> perhaps a bed on the floor. That is where the old people
> slept, close to the fire. These houses were made of stones
> and mortar, many of them with only a rough finish, because
> they were built in haste with everyone taking a hand. The
> roof was made of rushes or reeds over a thick, stout layer
> of scraws.

An tOileánach

In later years the thatch was replaced by tarred felt and outhouses
were built for the animals.

These houses were hardly less primitive than the prehistoric
beehive huts (*clocháin*) still to be seen in the west of Ireland. They
are used now, if at all, as cattle shelters. We know of one Blasket
family that actually lived in a *clochán*. In 1838 a traveller named
John Windele, accompanied by the parish priest, paid a visit to
Inish Tooskert, the most rugged and inaccessible of all the Blaskets. There he found a *clochán*, just over eleven feet in diameter,
occupied by Tomás O'Keane with his wife and eight children.
They were the only inhabitants of the island. The visitor was
hospitably received by the woman of the house, who insisted on
presenting him with a parting gift.

The real cause of the Famine lay in the Industrial Revolution,
already far advanced in Britain and North America. In Britain

the capital came largely from the colonies and dependencies over-seas; in America from the profits of large-scale agriculture. It was in these years that Britain became "the workshop of the world". The growth of large-scale manufacture and mechanised transport created an inexhaustible demand for cheap labour, which in turn demanded cheap food. The Corn Laws were repealed and the market was thrown open to imports from the new grain-growing areas of North America and Australia. Accordingly, the Irish farmers turned from grain to beef, and the smallholders were evicted to clear the land for pasture. The dispossessed peasants emigrated to seek employment overseas, leaving the Irish plains free for the development of large-scale agriculture. Thus, drained of both capital and labour, Ireland remained economically backward.

Meanwhile the fishing industry was re-organised. With improved communications by land and sea, the market for fresh fish, especially mackerel and lobster, was expanding. The sailing smack was replaced by the steam trawler. These developments were not available to the inshore fisherman, who lacked capital, but he too improved his methods. Hitherto the Islanders had possessed two large smacks, each with a crew of eight and owned jointly by them, together with a number of smaller craft. These were now abandoned in favour of the canvas-covered canoe or currach (*naomhóg*) manned by three or four men. This type of craft, which had been in use for centuries further up the coast, was preferred to the sailing smack because it was light and easy to handle, and hence better suited to the work of laying and drawing lobster pots.

These changes led to others, and there followed a period of prosperity such as the Islanders had not enjoyed before. In 1879-80 there had been a recurrence of famine conditions, which the Government relieved by the free distribution of Indian meal. This was followed a few years later by a reduction of the rent. Thanks to good catches of fish and stable prices, the standard of living rose. New habits were formed and old ones discarded. Many articles of consumption – tea, flour, sugar, cutlery, crockery – which had previously been luxuries, came now to be regarded as necessities. The hunting of seals (for which the hunter was equipped with nothing but a wooden club and a rope) was abandoned; the spinning-wheel fell into disuse; the cresset of fish-oil was replaced by the paraffin lamp; the girls began buying print frocks. All these changes, bringing with them greater dependence on the market, took place in the lifetime of Tomás.

The prosperity was short-lived. It was not long before fleets of steam-trawlers appeared in the Blasket waters, scouring the sea-bed and ranging ever further afield as the stocks of fish were depleted. The inshore fisherman, with only a canoe, was no match for the big companies now competing fiercely among themselves in the uncontrolled expansion of deep-sea fishing. In the year 1921 there were 400 canoes in the district west of Dingle; in 1934 there were only 80. In this as in other industries there was no future for small-scale production.

Looking back over his life, Tomás describes the hazards of seine fishing in a small boat:

> Often we put out to sea in fair weather at dawn, and when we returned the people were keening for us, the day had turned out so foul. Often we had to be out at night, and the misery of that kind of fishing cannot be described. I count it the worst of all trades that ever I set hand or foot to: the rollers towering overhead and shutting out the sight of land; a long, cold night battling against heavy seas, and often with little profit, just praying from one moment to the next for the help of God. It is seldom we got a haul sufficient for our needs, and even then we might have to cut the nets, which we had bought so dear, and leave them, fish and all, to drift away with the tide. On other nights, the boats would be nicely full after all our toil, but then we could not make harbour or land with the swell rising up over the green grass in a north-westerly gale and the surf sweeping over the rocks in every stretch of the sea. We would then have to run under sail before the wind, some of us to Crooked Creek, others to Ventry Harbour or Dingle; then home in the teeth of the storm, then out again the next night on the bank where our livelihood was.
>
> *An tOileánach*

Each member of the crew knew that the others held his life in their hands. Solidarity was a condition of survival.

In the years following the First World War, which brought famine to many parts of Europe, the fishing industry was disrupted by violent fluctuations of supply and demand, from which the inshore fisherman was the first to suffer:

All along the coast every canoe was up to the chin with mackerel. In Smerwick Harbour the seine-nets were down to the sea-bed with fish. The sight of all the fish on its way to Dingle was a marvel to behold. A good part of it was bought at a shilling a hundred. That was not enough to pay for the cartage; it was sixpence short. The man who had caught the fish did not get even that shilling – no, not a penny of it. Not a single sixpence came into the Island for that day's fishing, though the boats were down to the gunwhale. The carters refused to take it; there was too much of it; it wouldn't pay. It couldn't be salted either. The salt-dealers had been charging a crown a hundred, but when they saw the people's plight, they charged fifteen shillings. So there was nothing left for it but to pick the fishes out of the nets and throw them back dead into the sea.

Allagar na hInise

Even before the war there were more Islanders in Springfield, Massachusetts than in the Island itself. Now the stream became a flood. In the old days only those who could not stay at home had emigrated; now, only those stayed who could not go.

A great change was coming over the Island. Since the fishing was gone under foot, all the young people were departing across to America, five or six of them together every year. Máire was not gone a couple of years when the passage money was sent across to Seán. A year after that Eibhlín went. Tomás Owen Vaun was gone already for some time, and he writing to me from beyond. My brother Mícheál was working for a tailor in Dingle, and there was nobody left now in the house but my grandfather, my father and myself.

Fiche Blian ag Fás

Mícheál would have gone, too, if he had not been a cripple.

The Land

In 1881, after prolonged agitation by the Land League, the Government passed a Land Act, which granted the peasants a reduction in the rent. This was the first step in the abolition of landlordism. The next was taken some twenty-five years later under a series of Land Acts. In 1910 an official of the newly constituted Congested Districts Board visited the Blasket Island and proposed a new deal to the tenants. The rents were to be abolished. Instead they were to pay an annual instalment – much less than the rent – of the market price of the land and, when that had been paid off, the land would be theirs. These proposals were welcomed by the Islanders and brought them great relief – although, of course, from a historical point of view they were buying what had once been their own.

As part of the new deal the official from the Board spent some time in the Island supervising a re-division of the fields. In this he was assisted by Tomás:

> A few days later, the officer from the Board moved in, set up his tent, and stayed with us a long time, measuring and dividing the land. I was at the other end of the chain. The Board tidied us up so that everyone knew what was his and could fence it in and sow it as and when he pleased.
>
> *An tOileánach*

An eye-witness of this historic change was Robin Flower, then on his first visit to the Island:

> The old medieval common-field system, under which one man owned strips of land scattered over the whole area in a fashion only identifiable by an expert in traditional lore, was giving way in a moment to the system under which each family has its own land in concentrated blocks of arable and pasture.
>
> *The Western Island*

The common-field system was derived from the primitive village community, which was based on a level of subsistence so low as to preclude economic inequalities. Each family held a holding in the land, which was cultivated collectively. The arable was divided into several fields, lying on different sides of the village, and each field was laid out in strips. The family holding consisted of several "parcels" of strips, one in each field, the size of the parcels being adjusted to the size of the family. This arrangement served to eliminate inequalities due to variable factors, such as the quality of the soil and the distance from the village; and at the same time, being unenclosed, the holdings could be reallocated from time to time to meet changing needs. In later times, however, when collective cultivation had been abandoned, the old lay-out in scattered strips became an encumbrance, wasteful of time and labour. Disputes between neighbours were frequent. Seán O'Crohan tells of the confusion caused by mischievous boys who used to remove the big stones that served as landmarks.[1] That was the situation in the Blasket in 1910.

Then, on the initiative of the Board, the land was divided in such a way that each tenant received two plots, one in the upper field and one in the lower, which he could fence in and cultivate as he pleased, because they were now his. This was a momentous event in the history of the Island, bringing with it a new spirit of independence, which Tomás put into words:

> This field belongs to Tomás O'Crohan. I am Tomás. It was given to me by the Congested Districts Board when they divided the land.
>
> *Allagar na hInise*

Contemplating his newly acquired property, he develops a

heightened consciousness of his individuality.

The Islanders continued to enjoy their rights of common. The best pastures were shared between groups of families, the rest of the grazing land was common. Each family had its own turf-cutting where the best turf was to be had; the rest was open to all.

The house went with the landholding. Both were transmitted from father to son by means of marriages designed to secure continuity of ownership.

> When the elder son reached marriageable age, he was obliged to take the wife his father had chosen for him, or else leave the house, and then the second son would have her. There was no question in those days of "slipping your hand under her arm and carrying her off". It was a wife from your father or no wife at all. So, of course, he took her. After being married for a year or two in the same house as his father and his two brothers, a new house would be built for him and his wife, and then the second son would marry in the old house. Then, when the time was up, he too would have a new house, leaving the old one to the third son.
>
> *Lá Dár Saol*

The Islanders were all poor, though some were better off than others. However, there were no distinctions of rank apart from the esteem earned by individual merit:

> In my young days the two leading men in the Island were Pádraig O'Keane and (some time before him) Pádraig O'Guiheen. I remember seeing this Pádraig O'Keane (grandfather of the present King) with four or five milch cows. I never saw O'Guiheen myself (his grandchildren were living in my time) but I often heard that he had eight or ten milch cows, a mare and a wooden plough.
>
> *An tOileánach*

We are told here that the grandson and namesake of this Pádraig O'Keane was known as the King. No special significance was attached to the title, which was regarded as a tribute to his fine physique and dignified bearing. Most of the old men had nicknames, and this was one of them. However, his position was an important one. He was the postman. Every Tuesday and Friday, weather permitting, he made the crossing to the mainland to despatch and collect the mail at the post-office in Dunquin.

He had good English, and on the mainland he represented the Islanders in any dealings they might have with the civic authorities. He was their accepted spokesman in the reception of strangers, and in earlier times, when visitors to the Island were few, they usually stayed at his house. He was the only one, apart from Tomás, to read the newspaper, which he brought in with the post; and the old men used to meet in one of the houses (known for that reason as Parliament House) to hear the news and discuss world affairs. All this gave him a measure of authority, which must have owed something to the prestige enjoyed by the family as one of the longest-established in the Island, reminding us of the village chief or headman in primitive communities in other parts of the world.

The Art of Storytelling

The language of the Blasket Islanders was Irish or Irish Gaelic, closely related to Scots Gaelic, more remotely to Welsh and Breton. These are all that remain of the Celtic group of languages, which were once spoken right across Europe from Asia Minor to the Atlantic. Irish is the most archaic of those that survive and contains some structural features that seem to be derived from pre-Celtic languages that have completely disappeared. It is also exceptionally rich in folk-tales.

The Irish folk-tales are usually divided into three categories. First, there are the heroic tales. These include the Ulster Cycle, which is current only in the north, and the Fenian Cycle, which is current in both north and south. Secondly, there are tales of local history, such as the stories relating to Pierce Ferriter. And thirdly, there are magical, religious and romantic tales.

Of the heroic tales, the Ulster Cycle treats of two central figures, Cú Chulainn and Deirdre. Cú Chulainn is the greatest of all warriors, who meets an untimely death but wins immortal glory. Deirdre, brought up as the king's bride-to-be, escapes to Scotland with the sons of Usna but is lured back by treachery and dies by her own hand.

The Fenian Cycle is concerned with the Fianna, or Fenians, a roving band of warriors and huntsmen led by Fionn Mac Cumhail. A woman named Gráinne, betrothed to Fionn, elopes

25

with Diarmaid son of Duibhne. After many adventures, which take them all over Ireland, Diarmaid is killed at a boar hunt and Gráinne returns to Fionn. In another tale we are told how the Fenians were hunting by Loch Léin at Killarney when Niamh, daughter of the King of Eternal Youth, appeared before them and invited Oisín (Usheen or Ossian) to go with her to the Land of the Young, where he would enjoy everlasting life. Oisín went and lived there many years, but eventually he returned and was transformed into a decrepit old man.

It is interesting to compare these tales with the Greek. They seem to have taken shape early in the Christian era, though they are largely pagan in content. They are, therefore, far less ancient than the Greek. On the other hand, they are still living on the lips of the people. Every educated Greek is familiar with Homeric tales of the Trojan War, but only from literary sources; for after the introduction of Christianity the pagan stories were forgotten by the common people. In Ireland, too, many were lost in this way, but others have survived in oral tradition down to our own day.

One of the best-known of the Fenian tales was located close to the Blasket. This was the story of the Battle of Ventry, in which the Fianna fought for a whole year against an invading host from France. In addition, there was a wealth of local and historical tales associated with the district. Sybil Head is named after a girl of the Ferriters who was drowned there after eloping with her lover. At Cuas an Bhodaigh (Churl's Cove) a woman lay with a phantom man who came up to her out of the sea, and gave birth to a son who never slept. A mermaid was sunning herself on the strand at Inch when she was captured by a man of the O'Shea family, who took her to wife. The whole landscape was steeped in legendary memories of the past.

The favourite pastimes of the Islanders were singing, dancing and storytelling. Often the three would be combined. A message would pass through the village that a dance was to be held that evening in a certain house, and when the time came a fiddler would strike up and the people gathered in. The fiddles were home-made, with sheep's gut for the strings. Then, after an hour or so of music and dancing, the stories would begin.

There were some good storytellers in the Island, men and women, one of whom has acquired an international reputation. This was Peig Sayers. She was born in Dunquin in 1873 but married into the Island and spent most of her life there. She was illiterate in Irish, and her stories were recorded from her by dictation or by dictaphone. There are over 5,000 manuscript pages of material collected from her in the archives of the Irish Folklore Commission.

The art of storytelling was not hereditary in any formal sense, but it was often so in practice because the storyteller's children were in the best position to acquire it. Peig learnt it from her father:

> My father had more tales than any man of his time, and if you had heard him telling them you would have wondered, for he never forgot anything but went right on, one thing after another, all the tale as it happened, and all the sayings and ways of speech, he had them all better than any other man. He lived to be ninety-six years old, and till a day or two before his death he could tell any tale without stopping or staying, and his mind was clear and his speech as good as it had ever been. He was a little, lively man, and the boys of the village used to come to our house over there in Dunquin at night to hear him storytelling.
>
> *The Western Island*

These tales opened up a fantastic world in which no distinction was drawn between the natural and the supernatural, because nature was so imperfectly known, a world peopled by hostile forces which could only be kept at bay by heroic deeds supported by faith in God. The people loved them all the more because they knew them so well, rejoicing and grieving with the hero and relishing every witty or well-turned phrase. Through them, shaped and re-shaped by accomplished craftsmen, the moral and cultural values of the community were conveyed to the rising generation from early childhood in an unconsciously artistic form.

So far we have been concerned only with stories conforming to the accepted definition of a folk-tale – that is, stories relating to a more or less distant past. There were also stories of another kind, taken from the storyteller's own life. These autobiographical tales, as they may be called, had always been popular and remained so even after the folk-tales proper had lost their appeal. Peig recalls how she used to spend the winter nights:

> Often, when the old man and I were seated rather lonesome

by the fire, with no one to interrupt, we used to tell each other a great many little stories to beguile the night away. He used to describe the hardships he had lived through and the perils he had encountered at sea.

Peig

Tomás O'Crohan recalls similar occasions:

My finger gave me a good deal of pain, and I had some trouble with it before it cleared up. Bald Tom used to spend the evenings with us till bedtime. He was fine company, and I did not feel the pain half as much while he was talking and telling of the hard life he had lived. My father was nearly as old as he was, but not half so good at remembering the past with all the incidental details.

An tOileánach

In these autobiographical tales the narrator recalls events of his own life, which he relates just as they occurred, except that he has re-shaped them to some extent in his imagination in order to make a good story out of them; and he does this with all the skill he has acquired, as practitioner or as listener, in the storyteller's art.

A good example is "Ventry Races" in *Twenty Years A-Growing*. Every incident is reproduced so concretely that it seems as though they are being enacted before our eyes. This sense of immediacy is characteristic of the folk-tale. The successive episodes are linked in such a way as to bind them together in an organic whole. The boys' delight at setting foot on the mainland turns to dismay when they find that the boat has left for home without them. Leaving Dunquin, they are "as light as a starling for the road", but on the way back they can "hardly put one foot before the other". The story of the inhospitable farmer is matched by their own reception at Ballykeen. The episodes are arranged rondo-like round the central event of the day, which is the fight with Cosey, likened to the Battle of Ventry. This cyclical structure is also found in the folk-tales. Thus, while the story itself is the author's own, the skill with which it is told is traditional.

Autobiographical tales of this kind are, of course, to be found everywhere, but in the Blasket Island they acquired a special importance because, owing to a unique combination of circumstances, they provided the link which led from the folk-tales to the books.

From Speech to Writing

The decline of the Irish language dates from the end of the seventeenth century. The Irish tribal system, deeply divided within itself, collapsed under the impact of the Cromwellian and Williamite wars, and Ireland became an English colony.

Under the Penal Laws, the Catholics, who formed the great majority of the population, were denied political rights, forbidden to practice their religion, and could only educate their children by sending them abroad. As the medium of administration and commerce, English gained ground steadily at the expense of Irish, which sank to the level of a patois. We hear of Irishmen living on the continent who were highly educated in the language of their adoption, yet were illiterate in their own language. The result was that the struggle for Catholic emancipation and the political movements that followed it were all conducted through English.

By the time Tomás O'Crohan was born, in 1856, the majority of the Irish people were English-speaking, though many of the rural areas were bilingual. Bilingualism brought the two languages into direct contact with one another. There developed a dialect of English in which all the deviations from the standard form of that language are due to the influence, conscious or unconscious, of Irish speech – English with an Irish substratum. At the same time the Irish of these areas lost much of its richness and elegance. It was only in the most remote and isolated districts, where English had not yet penetrated, that the native language preserved its full vigour and purity. The Blasket was one of these.

In 1893 the Gaelic League was founded. Its aim was to revive the language together with other forms of Irish culture, such as music and dancing, which had fallen into neglect under English rule. It received enthusiastic support, especially from young people, and not only from the Catholic majority. Its founder, Douglas Hyde, and other prominent members belonged to the Protestant Ascendancy, whose ancestors had never been Irish-speaking. For them, too, it was a liberating force. Without this source of inspiration the literary renaissance associated with the names of Yeats, Synge and Lady Gregory could not have taken place. This was an enduring achievement, but not what had been intended. Ironically, it was in the Irish-speaking areas that the movement had least success. It did nothing to stem the tide of emigration, which was depopulating the West. For the peasants who still spoke it the language was a mark of poverty and backwardness, which they were determined to shake off. They insisted that their children should learn English and suspected some Gaelic Leaguers of being more concerned for the language than for the people that spoke it:

> Great God of Virtues! the chatter and gabble of the people! And not a word of Irish to be heard! I don't know what in the world brings strangers to the Blasket to learn Irish – for, so far as I can see, when they come back here, after leaving the Island, they have it thrown under foot. Look at myself now! What would I do if there was not a word of English on my own lips? Wouldn't I be a public show? Where is the man or woman who would give me an answer? Will the day ever come when Irish will be poured out here as English is today? I doubt it.
>
> *Fiche Blian ag Fás*

Another by-product of the language revival was the development of Irish scholarship. Old and Middle Irish were already subjects of study in Dublin and in several continental universities, and a number of foreign scholars now took an interest in the vernacular. They were attracted to the south-west, where the literary tradition was best preserved in the local dialects, and in particular, for the reasons already mentioned, to the Great Blasket Island. There they became pupils and friends of Tomás O'Crohan. Among them were Carl Marstrander from Norway, Carl Wilhelm von Sydow from Sweden, Robin Flower, George Thomson and Kenneth Jackson from England, Marie Sjoestedt-Jonval from France. The Islanders took these strangers to their hearts. They welcomed them all the more warmly because of their own traditional respect for poetry and scholarship, and, in return for teaching them the language, they learnt from them that their island was one of the last homes of an ancient civilisation which, though now on the verge of extinction, had preserved certain values which the modern world had lost.

Marstrander visited the Blasket in 1907 and spent five months there. Flower paid his first visit in 1910 and took down from Tomás a number of local-historical tales, which were published in 1956 as *Seanchas ón Oileán Tiar*. Meanwhile, Tomás had become interested in the Gaelic League, which had started language classes in Dunquin. Detained for a few days by bad weather, he picked up a textbook and brought it home with him. From it he taught himself to read and write. Then, in 1917-18, another visitor, a schoolmaster from Killarney named Brian O'Kelly (Brian Ó Ceallaigh), spent a whole year in the Blasket. It was he who persuaded Tomás to write his autobiography, giving him just the guidance that he needed in order to acquire the art of writing without detriment to the oral tradition in which he had been brought up. This was a turning point in Tomás's life. For several years he kept a journal, which was published in 1928 as *Allagar na hInise* and in 1986 as *Island Cross-Talk*. It consists mainly of conversation pieces which reveal the medieval mentality of the old people and their delight in displaying their command of the spoken word. Then, completed in 1926 and published in 1929, came his autobiography *An tOileánach*, with an English edition – *The Islandman* – in 1934. In the last chapter he wrote:

> Never, since the first fire was lit on this island, has anyone written about his life and times. I am proud to have set down in writing the story of myself and my neighbours. It will tell people how the Islanders lived in the old days.
>
> *An tOileánach*

Tomás led the way and others followed. The next generation – the last – was literate in both languages, both being now taught at school. Muiris O'Sullivan's *Fiche Blian ag Fás*, or *Twenty Years A-Growing,* was followed by Peig Sayers' two volumes, written down by her son Mícheál O'Guiheen, who also produced three books of his own, including a volume of poems. Then came several more autobiographies and a collection of letters written in English. Add to these a phrase-book of the local dialect and a topographical description of the Islands, both by Tomás, and we have a little library of seventeen volumes. Of course, they are not all of equal value, but together they provide a unique account of life in a remote village community written by the villagers themselves. What is the secret of their success?

These authors were all versed to a greater or lesser degree in the art of storytelling. Their mode of speech and their outlook on life had been moulded by the traditional tales which they had inherited from past generations. What they did, therefore, was to select from their own experience a number of episodes which they had already cultivated as fireside tales and arrange them as a continuous narrative. In their hands, therefore, the transition from speech to writing was effected without a break. The magic of the fireside tale was carried over into print.

The conclusion is confirmed when we consider the subject matter of the books. There is nothing in the way of life which they describe that could not be paralleled in other Gaelic-speaking communities in Ireland or Scotland, or indeed in many peasant communities all over the world, but nowhere else has that way of life been portrayed by people who were actually living it and knew no other. In that respect these books are unique. This consideration applies above all to Tomás and to Peig, neither of whom ever set foot beyond Tralee, but it is hardly less true of Muiris, who did travel as far as Dublin but never succeeded in emancipating himself (if that is the right word) from the values of his own society.

However, as literacy spread, the old tales were forgotten.

One of the finest storytellers in the Island was Seán Eoin O'Donlevy (Seán Fada or Long John, as he was called). He had a magnificent repertory of heroic tales, but in his last years he was forgetting them. Talking to Robin Flower he said:

> "It was only the other day that I had all the old tales in my mind, and I could have spent the night telling them to you without a word out of place in any tale. But now I

couldn't tell a tale of them. And do you know what has driven them out of my mind?"

"Well, I suppose you are losing your memory," I said.

"No, it isn't that, for my memory is as good as it ever was for other things. But it is Tomás that has done it, for he has books and newspapers, and he reads them to me; and the little tales, one after another, day after day, in the books and newspapers, have driven the old stories out of my head. But maybe I am little the worse for losing them."

The Western Island

Improvised Verse

If we discount the visits of Pierce Ferriter, the only poets we have had in the Island, so far as people can remember, were Seán O'Donlevy and his contemporary, Mícheál O'Sullivan.[1]

Both belonged to the last century. A good many of Seán's pieces have been preserved and edited, but from Mícheál we have only a few stanzas. In addition, the Islanders had inherited from the eighteenth century two long narrative poems – *The Lay of Oisín in the Land of the Young* and *The Midnight Court* – together with a mass of occasional poetry: songs of praise, wedding songs, elegies, satires, lampoons, gnomic quatrains, etc. This poetical tradition had been maintained in earlier times by bards attached to the local chiefs, like the court minstrels of other lands. After the Battle of the Boyne in 1690 the last of the chiefs fled to the continent and the bards were scattered among the peasantry.

It might have been thought that under the Penal Laws the art of poetry would have been extinguished but, on the contrary, it flourished. There arose a new school of poets who depended for their livelihoods on the people and so were able to combine bardic sophistication with peasant vitality. The greatest of them were Aogán O'Rahilly (1675-1729) and Eoghan Rua O'Sullivan (1748-84), both born near Killarney. They were well organised:

Scholarly semi-professionals still subsisted in large numbers

34

in rural communities during the eighteenth and early nineteenth centuries. On occasions throughout the year, where literary traditions were strongest, they gathered together in "courts of poetry", recited their compositions, exchanged manuscripts, and engaged in extempore repartee in verse. As time, and the conquest, proceeded, it is their voices that emerged more and more as the voice of their community.

An Duanaire 1600-1900

A reminiscence of that time, when poetry belonged to the people, has been preserved by Tomás O'Crohan in the following anecdote:

It was the day of the horse fair at Castleisland near Killarney. At the entrance to the paddock there stood a farmer named Power. He had just returned home after spending twenty years in America, where he had done well. He was now making himself known to his old friends as they entered the paddock. As the first of them approached, he addressed him in verse with a quatrain. Then, at his suggestion, his friend addressed the next comer in the same way, one after another improvising a quatrain until there were six of them. Shortly afterwards, a member of the local gentry who happened to be passing, approached the six, who were now surrounded by a large crowd, eager to hear more poetry, and he offered a prize of five pounds to the one who would deliver himself of the best quatrain in praise of his horse. The prize went to Power, who ordered drinks all round.

Seanchas ón Oileán Tiar

Tomás records all the quatrains – the six recited at the paddock gate and the six recited before the crowd. Read in cold print they are not very impressive except as exercises in virtuosity, but they should be judged in their context. They were not composed for posterity but to enhance the enjoyment of the moment. The men who composed them were not professional poets. They belonged to a community in which everyone spoke with a keen sense of style, even in everyday conversation, and under the stress of emotion they expressed themselves freely in metrical forms. The delight in poetry was universal and so it could still draw a crowd. Perhaps the best comment on this story is provided by a poem of Yeats inspired by Galway Races, where he might well have encountered an incident of the same kind:

> There where the course is,
> Delight makes all of the one mind,
> The riders upon the galloping horses,
> The crowd that closes in behind:
> We, too, had good attendance once,
> Hearers and hearteners of the work;
> Aye, horsemen for companions,
> Before the merchant and the clerk
> Breathed on the world with timid breath.
>
> Sing on: somewhere at some new moon
> We'll learn that sleeping is not death,
> Hearing the whole earth change its tune,
> Its flesh being wild, and it again
> Crying aloud as the racecourse is,
> And we find hearteners among men
> That ride upon horses.
>
> *W.B. Yeats: "At Galway Races"*

Tomás himself composed a number of poems, some of which were current for many years, but he did not improvise, and in the next generation the practice ceased. Gnomic quatrains were common and it was not always easy to tell whether they were original or derivative. The following is a case in point.

Muiris O'Sullivan is in Inish Vickillaun and he is examining some names and dates carved in stone by visitors a couple of centuries before.

> At that moment a verse came into my head and I recited it to Pádraig:
> "The trout lives in the stream,
> The duck lives on the strand,
> The blossom lives on the tree,
> But not the writer's hand."
>
> *Fiche Blian ag Fás*

The idea is that animal and plant life renews itself endlessly without any apparent change, but the men who carved those names and dates have gone for ever. Was Muiris extemporising when he said this, or had he heard it from his grandfather? Most probably the latter.

A similar idea occurs in one of Thomas Hardy's lyrics:

> A bird sings the selfsame song,
> With never a fault in its flow
> That we listened to hear those long
>> Long years ago.
>
> A pleasing marvel is how
> A strain of such rapturous rote
> Should have gone on thus till now
>> Unchanged in a note!
>
> But it's not the selfsame bird –
> No: perished to dust is he!
> As also are those who heard
>> That song with me.

The poem is Hardy's own, but the idea may have been traditional; for he too was a peasant poet.

The truth is that, in criticising the poetry of a pre-literate community, the concept of originality is scarcely applicable. All such poetry is derivative in the sense that it is drawn from tradition. It is original only in so far as the individual recreates it in response to his personal experience. Such poetry may attain a high technical level, like any other village craft, but its intellectual scope is necessarily limited. With the weakening of communal ties the poet loses the faculty of improvisation but at the same time becomes conscious of his individuality.

Such a poet was Mícheál O'Guiheen who, after the evacuation of the Island, spent his last years living alone in the shadow of Mount Eagle. Here is one of his religious poems. Although divided into quatrains, it is non-metrical – a sort of free verse or rhythmical prose. The translation here is a prose version.

> Hail, calm Virgin; hail, face without guile; hail star of the light, glory and joy of the children of Israel!
>
> Mother of sorrow and grief, who received the call above all women; virgin who suffered with patience; brilliant flower in the sight of God!
>
> We pray to thee in the mysterious stillness of the night, that God's happiness may be brought into our midst, saving

us from wrong.

From swirling cross-currents in a sea of pains, O God,
deliver the sinners of the world. Mary, take us by the
hand to a place which I have never seen.

Hell it is to me to be alive, walking this road without God.
Is there anyone today beneath the sun more pitiful than
I at the day's end?

Mary, is it not I who played false with God's glorious gifts?
He gave me long life and health, and see how I have
spent them!

I am praying to thee tonight, Mary, alone beside the fire.
The greatness of my grief is known to none but thee.
Grant me respite, Mary, who never failed yet, may I
spend in righteousness the time that God has granted me.

Coinnle Corra

Mícheál was a humble craftsman in a small community. He
was not a great poet, but his work conforms to the poet's essential
task as defined by Goethe – namely, to put into words what
others feel but cannot express for themselves:

Nature has left us tears, the cry of pain,
When man can bear no more, and most of all
To me – she has left me melody and speech
To make the full depth of my anguish known;
And when man in his agony is dumb,
I have God's gift to utter what I suffer.

Goethe: "Tasso"

The Prose Poems

The Blasket books have certain features in common with the Homeric poems. Those poems took shape out of shorter lays which had been transmitted orally over many centuries, and thanks to an exceptionally favourable combination of historical conditions the transition from speech to writing was effected so skilfully that many characteristic features of oral recitation were carried over into written literature. Among these were the use of ornamental epithets and set passages repeated without variation to describe recurrent situations, such as starting out on a journey, preparing for battle, partaking of a meal, and so on.

There are also, of course, important differences. In the historical period the Homeric poems were recited, not sung. In earlier times they had been chanted by a minstrel accompanying himself on the lyre. The Gaelic tales were in prose, but it was a special kind of prose with many poetical features, including those just noted in the Homeric poems. It had been customary at an earlier period for the narrator to insert from time to time a short lyrical poem appropriate to the situation. All these features can be traced in the Blasket books.

A typical example of these conventional formulas, employed both in the traditional and in the autobiographical tales, is the following:

We turned stern to land and prow to sea, hoisted sail and set out for the west with a fair breeze behind us.

An tOileánach

We took oars and sail aboard and set prow to sea and stern to land, as they did in the old tales long ago.

An tOileánach

Soon we had turned our faces to the island and our backs to the Wild Bank.

Fiche Blian ag Fás

In the last instance the formula is inverted, because the men are rowing and therefore facing the other way. Other examples (not always easy to translate, because some of the epithets are alliterative or archaic):

If it be no better, let it be no worse.

They made neither stop nor stay.

Without care, concern or complaint.

We were discussing and debating the ways of the world.

He received the choicest of food and drink and a bed to sleep in.

In addition there are many allusions to incidents in the heroic tales:

They were scattered like the children of Lir.

As hard on her subjects as Queen Maeve in Connacht long ago.

The black curses that Fionn put on the limpets.

These formulas were all part of the storyteller's stock-in-trade and were often to be heard in ordinary conversation. They show how the forms of popular speech had been moulded by the storyteller's art.

The Islanders enjoyed nothing so much as conversation, which they liked to adorn with proverbial couplets and quatrains ("as the poet said long ago"); or they might introduce from the same source some image or idea as though it was their own. This was all the easier because the thoughts embodied in their poetry were their thoughts.

Muiris is chatting idly with his grandfather one sunny morning in the hills:

> My grandfather and I were lying on Castle Summit. It was a fine sunny day in July. The sun was splitting the stones with heat and the grass burnt to the roots. I could see far away to the south Iveragh painted in many colours by the sun. South-west were the Skelligs, glistening white, and the sea around them dotted with fishing boats from England. "Isn't it a fine healthy life those fishermen have, daddo," said I.
>
> I got no answer. Turning round, I saw the old man was asleep. I looked at him, thinking. You were once in the flower of youth, said I in my own mind, but my sorrow, the skin of your brow is wrinkled now, and the hair on your head is grey. You are without suppleness in your limbs and without interest in the grand view to be seen from this hill. But alas, if I live, I will be one day as you are now.
>
> *Fiche Blian ag Fás*

The Islanders had a quatrain, which they attributed to Pierce Ferriter. It ran as follows:

> Look on this head agape with holes for eyes,
> And look how bare this toothless jawbone is!
> Look, too, for all your strength and beauty now,
> The day shall come when yours shall be like this.

The boy's thoughts have been shaped in form and content by the quatrain. In addition to such echoes of popular poetry, the Blasket books contain a large number of extended passages descriptive of natural phenomena, all constructed on similar lines, with nothing to distinguish them from poetry proper except the lack of metrical form. Examples of these "prose poems", as they may be called, are to be found in Tomás, Muiris and Peig. In *Twenty Years A-Growing* they are integrated with the narrative in such a way as to display the ever-changing panorama of nature as a background to the activities of man.

Let us begin with a passage from Tomás. (The titles have been added by the present writer.)

A Winter's Day

It is a winter's day and looks it. The blast of the great gale is driving the waves over everything within reach. The rocks out to sea are hidden from sight by the squalls of white surf bursting over them. Grass that was green yesterday is withered today. Even the people's skins are changing in the bad weather. Sheep that have been blown out of their resting-places in the hills are trying to force their way into the houses. The fish that lay all summer basking on the top of the water have vanished in the storm. The young woman who at other times was as spruce as the swan on the lake, when she comes in with a bucket of water, the comb has been snatched by the wind from the back of her head, her hair has strayed into her mouth, she has mud on her clothes, the water is half spilt, and she is as grumpy as one who is out of tobacco. Of the old people whose limbs had been so fine and supple in the warmth of the sun, one has a shrivelled leg, another complains of his arm, and another is dozing over the fire, and they are keeping an eye on him lest he should fall into it.

There are many cures in fine weather and much harm in bad.

Allagar na hInise

There follow three examples from Muiris:

A Stormy Day

I had now spent a month on the sea, as happy as a prince returning home in the evening and setting out with the chirp of the sparrow. But one day, when we were out as usual, I noticed a difference. The fine view was not to be seen, there was no gladness in my heart, the birds were not singing nor the seal sunning himself on the ledge, no heron, ring-plover or sea-pie was at the water's edge picking the limpets, no path of gold in the Bay of Dingle nor ripples glittering in the sunshine, no sultry haze in the bosom of the hills, no rabbits to be seen with ears cocked on the clumps of thrift. A gale was blowing from the south, and where the water lapped before, the waves were now hurling themselves with a roar against the rocks, not a bird's cry to be heard but all of them cowering in their holes, big clouds sweeping across the sky ready to burst with the weight of the rain, the wind howling through the coves, the bright flowers above me twisted together in the storm, and no delight in my heart but cold and distress.

Fiche Blian ag Fás

Greeting The Sun

It was a beautiful morning, a streak of light across Cnoc an Choma in the east and everything coming to life. The sheep which had been sitting in the furrow in the run of the night rose and stretched itself. The folded leaf was opening. The hen which had hidden her head under her wing was crying gob-gob-gob to be let out into the fields. Birds, beast and man were waking to pay homage to the sun. A moment before not a sound was to be heard but now the birds were singing, the cow, the sheep, the ass and even man himself throwing up their snatches of song.

Fiche Blian ag Fás

Nightfall

It was growing late. The sun was sinking on the horizon, the dew falling heavily as the air cooled, the dock leaves closing up for the night, the birds crying as they came back to their young, rabbits rushing through the fern as they left the warrens, the sparkle gone out of the Kerry diamonds, and a lonesome look coming over the ravines. "It is night, Tomás."

Fiche Blian ag Fás

These passages embody the deep-seated belief in the kinship of man and nature, both subject to the same cycle of day and night, summer and winter, birth and death. This is a prominent feature of Gaelic poetry.

Further, when compared with one another and with other passages of the same kind, they are seen to be constructed on the same lines.

The weather signs are described one by one, in no apparent order but more or less at random, just as they strike the eye or ear. The same formulas are used repeatedly to point the contrast between past and present ("That which was A is now B"; "It is no longer A but B" etc). Sentences are strung together, each beginning with the same verb, affirmative or negative. Many of the pieces conclude by summing up the significance of the whole or by repeating a word or idea from the beginning.

These passages are so striking in themselves and at the same time so similar to one another that we are impelled to look for some common source. We have already noted that some of the heroic tales go back to pagan times, and that they had once included recitations of lyric poetry. The chief glory of ancient Irish literature is its nature poetry, consisting of short lyrics portraying some aspect of nature and put into the mouth of one of the heroic characters. Of these lyrics Kuno Meyer wrote:

> It is characteristic of these poems that in none of them do we get an elaborate or sustained description of any scene or scenery but rather a succession of pictures or images, which the poet, like an impressionist, calls up before us by light and skilful touches.
>
> *Selections From Ancient Irish Poetry*

This comment might have been written on the Blasket pieces.

The following lyric dates from the ninth century. The story to which it belonged has been lost, but it is said to have been recited by Fionn Mac Cumhail:

> I bring you news.
> > The stag is lowing.
> Winter descends.
> > Summer is gone.
> The wind is high and cold.
> > The sun is low.
> Short his course.
> > The sea is rising.
>
> The bracken has turned red.
> > Its shape is hidden.
> The wild goose has raised
> > Its wonted cry.
> The cold has gripped
> > The birds' wings.
> Season of ice,
> > That is my news.
>
> *Golden Treasury of Irish Verse, no 21*

The second piece is from the tenth or eleventh century. Diarmaid and Gráinne have taken shelter with an old woman on the hill of Howth, and she is urging them not to venture out that night.

Cold, cold!
  Cold tonight is the plain of Moylorg.
The snows are higher than the hills.
  Deer cannot reach their food.

Cold for ever!
  The storm sweeps over everything.
Every sloping furrow is a stream,
  Every ford a lake in flood,

Every lake a surging sea,
  Every pond a swollen lake.
No path for horses through Ross Ford,
  Even less for a pair of feet.

The fish of Ireland are on the move,
  No beach unbattered by the waves,
No badger in all the countryside,
  No rock is visible, no heron calls.

No sleep nor rest for the wolves of Cuan,
  Snowbound in their forest lairs;
No shelter for the little wren
  To build her nest on Blackbird Hill.

Hapless the flock of little birds
  In the grip of wind and ice.
The blackbird cannot find a nook
  In all Kilcoon to lay his breast.

Our pot hangs snugly on the hearth
  But the blackbird is homeless in Lettercrow.
Key wood is buried deep in drifts
  There's no one now could climb Ben Bow.

The eagle of heather-clad Glen Ree
  Suffers cruelly in the gale,
Wincing as the biting blast
  Drives drops of ice into his maw.

Do not rise from your downy bed!
  Mark my words, it would make no sense.

All the fords are frozen fast.
    That is why I am crying "Cold"!
        Golden Treasury of Irish Verse, no 31

Like the Blasket pieces these lyrics are devoted to the diurnal and annual changes of nature and their effects on man. They reveal the same lack of order in the presentation of details, the same insistent contrast between what was and what is, the same repetition of initial words, and the same link – the *ceangal* – between beginning and end. These resemblances are too close to be fortuitous. They show that the passages in question are formed on a traditional pattern which goes back to Old Irish nature poetry.

This conclusion is confirmed when we turn to another class of nature poetry – the valedictory poem, in which the poet bids farewell to some hill or valley where he has lived happily. The best known is Deirdre's farewell to Scotland.

Dear to me is that country to the east,
Alba, land of wonders.
I would never have come away,
Had I not come with Naoise.

Dear to me Dún Fidga and Dún Finn,
And the fortress that stands above them,
Dear to me is Sloe-tree Island,
Dear to me, too, Dún Sweeney.

Forest of Kilcoon!
Where Ainnle used to roam, alas!
All too short the time I spent
With Naoise in the land of Alba.

Glen Lay!
There I slept under a shady rock.
Fish and venison and badger's fat
Were my portion in Glen Lay.

Glen Massan!
How tall the wild garlic grows!
Fitful was our sleep at night
Above the marshy firth of Massan.

Glen Eitche!

It was there I set up my first house
In a lovely glade. At early rising
A sunny sheepfold was Glen Eitche.

Glen Urchain!
The vale runs straight between two hills.
Never was man prouder in his time
Than Naoise in Glen Urchain.

Glen Darua!
Greetings to all whose heritage it is!
Sweet the cuckoo's voice on the arched bough
In the hills above Glen Darua.

Dear to me is Sloe-tree Island,
Dear its sandy water.
I would never have come away,
Had I not come with my dearest.

Measgra Dánta, no 44

Oisín revisits the scene he had frequented with the Fianna in his youth:

I am sad at heart, Ben Goolan,
    Mountain of shapely peaks.
Before the coming of Patrick
    It was splendid to stand on your summit.

Many the hounds and the huntsmen
    That crowded your slopes, Ben Goolan.
Many the stalwart heroes
    That heard the melodious hunting horn. . .

Measgra Dánta, no 39

Reading these poems one can hardly fail to recall the passage in which Peig, looking across from the Blasket, addresses Mount Eagle:

O Mount Eagle, what a stately, noble figure is yours today!
Held fast in the grip of the years, you show no sign of age,
your form is as pleasing as ever. In the days of my childhood
there was no place under the bright sun that was brighter
to me, but now we are parted by the wide waters of the sea.

Machnamh Seanmhná

When Muiris landed in Dunquin on the start of his journey

47

to Dublin, he looked back at the Island and composed this quatrain, little knowing what a long history lay behind it:

> You are there, hill-top fair,
>   Ancient summit crowned with heath,
> While one who once ran races there
>   Looks back on you with grief.

Fiche Blian ag Fás

Some scholars believe that Irish nature poetry is derived from Druidical rites connected with the cycle of the seasons. If so, this type of poetry is as old as the heroic tales. How the lyrics came to be incorporated in the tales is not clear; perhaps they were designed, like the Homeric similes, to provide momentary relaxations of attention. It seems that the lyrical element, cultivated by the bards attached to the chiefs, dropped out of the storytelling as practised by the lower classes, until, when the courts broke up, it was transmitted to the peasantry in a non-metrical form.

The Blasket people had another type of prose poem, which differs from the preceding in that it follows no structural pattern. This was the improvised prayer, in which they poured out their hearts in language of the purest poetry. The example that follows is one that Peig heard from a woman known as Grey Bridie, a sister of her father's father. Bridie lost her husband and her eight children in the Famine. After burying the last of them with her own hands in the churchyard at Ballynahow, she blessed them:

> Rest in peace, dear children and gentle husband, in peace for ever more. You need have no fear of wakening till the sea flows from the north and the raven turns shining white. Do not be afraid of hunger or thirst, dear children, because you may quench your thirst today by drinking your fill from the stream of glory. I leave you at rest in God's grace till the Angel sounds the trumpet on the last day.

Peig

The Aisling

The dispersal of the bards brought about many changes in the art of poetry. The syllabic quatrain gave way to the accentual quatrain, which was closer to common speech. The compact style of the preceding period gave way to the more expansive movement of the folk-song. Some new genres were created. Among these was the *aisling*, which is the subject of the present chapter.

The word *aisling* ("vision") was used to denote a special type of song, which was highly cultivated by the peasant poets of the eighteenth century. In origin it was the Gaelic version of the medieval love-song, which was current in most parts of Western Europe. The poet goes out into the country, where he meets a fair maid who greets him and converses with him:

> Through bushes and through briars
>   Of late I took my way
> All for to hear the small birds sing
>   And the lambs to skip and play.
>
> I overheard my own true love,
>   Her voice it was so clear.
> Long time I have been waiting for
>   The coming of my dear. . .

The *aisling* was sung to a folk-tune, but it deviates in type in

one particular. Most of these poets were Jacobites and they identified the "fair maid" as Éire, who laments her subjection to
foreign rule and foretells the coming of her deliverer. This theme,
repeated with very little variation from poem to poem, is a
stereotype. What captures our attention is not the content of the
poem but the form, that is, the language, of which the best of
these poets display an astonishing mastery, drawing on all its
resources – rhythmical, melodic, syntactical. It is as though in
these poems content has become form and form content. That
is their unique quality. There is nothing like them in English
poetry. Their overall effect has been described by Donal O'Sullivan:

> Even in the humble folk poetry the effect is mellifluous and
> pleasing; but in the hands of a master the rich, flowing
> rhythms, varied harmonies, and untroubled ease of echo
> and reminiscences are something to marvel at, the result
> being a kind of poetry that is not merely made for music,
> but is in a certain sort music itself.
>
> *Songs of the Irish*

By way of example we quote an *aisling* by Mícheál O'Guiheen,
which must be the shortest, and perhaps the last, of its kind. All
the details are traditional. The "fair maid" is not identified, but
apart from that the poem conforms to type.

> I was strolling alone on a fine sunny morning, at peace with
> the world and nothing to trouble my heart, when I saw
> standing beside me a young woman, friendly and full of
> charm, her hair flowing in swathes down to the tips of
> the heather.

> I sat down on a green grassy bank, and – truth to tell – my
> heart leapt, for I thought to myself she could not be a
> woman of this world, and I feared some trickery.

> She wore a cloak of costly cloth with a sheen of heather
> blue, and had snatched the prize for grace and beauty
> from the women of all lands.

> We sat down together at one another's pleasure on the
> heather bank, and conversed happily together till the sun
> had stolen past its summit.

Oh, it is my grief that she was not still with me on that mossy bank at sunset.

Coinnle Corra

The *aisling* was sometimes used as an introduction to narrative poems. *The Midnight Court* begins with what is in effect an *aisling*, and in the *Lay Of Oisín* the hero begins his story in the same way.

The Midnight Court is a satire directed against the late marriages customary at the time.

It was my habit to stroll on the fresh green sward of a riverside meadow steeped in dew, at the edge of a wood in the folds of a mountain, carefree and sprightly, at the break of day.

It gladdened my heart to set eyes on Lough Graney, the lake and the landscape, and on the sunlit horizon the mountains set in a huddle together, nodding their heads from behind one another.

It would gladden the heart of an embittered pauper, bent double with trouble and the ills of old age, to pause for a while and look down over the tree-tops to the lake below, where a bevy of ducks, with a swan moving among them, are trailing across the cloudless bay.

The fish are rising, leaping for joy, and before my eyes a perch displays his dappled underside. The lake has many colours, as blue-grey billows stumble noisily onto the strand.

Birds make merry in the trees, a doe skips about in a copse close by, as the hunt crowds into view, with horns blowing, hounds baying in swift pursuit, and Reynard on the run.

At this point the poet falls asleep, and there appears before him, not the "fair maid", but a hideous old hag who drags him off to the fairies' court on the charge of remaining unwed.

Oisín tells of how the Fianna were deer-hunting one sunny morning on the banks of Loch Léin, when the goddess Niamh appeared before them in a blaze of light, riding a white horse and bearing down on them from the west.

At the sight of that queenly figure they called off the hunt and gazed at her in amazement, for they had never seen so fine a woman. She wore on her head a royal crown, with a brown mantle of costly silk, studded with stars, which covered her shoes right down to the tips of the grass.

From every tress of her golden hair hung a golden ringlet; her eyes were a clear and cloudless blue, like dew-drops on the grass.

Her cheeks were redder than the rose, her skin whiter than the swan on the wave; her lips were sweeter to the taste than honey drunk in red wine.

In these narrative poems the ornamentation is too lavish for our taste. Constantly repeated, the similes lose their effect. In skilful hands, however, they can be resuscitated. To illustrate this point let us turn back to *A Winter's Day*.

The details of that picture are all taken from the view which Tomás had before him all his life – with one exception. The bedraggled girl who brings in the bucket of water is said to have been at other times "as spruce as the swan on the lake". There are no swans in the Blasket Islands, and indeed it is doubtful if he had ever seen one. He was thinking of Niamh (see above) and of all the other "swan-women" (*eala-mhná*) whose praises had been sung by the poets. It is an imaginative touch, which for a moment transforms this peasant girl into a queen.

It is characteristic of a culture based on oral transmission that the poet can play on our feelings by alluding indirectly to traditional ideas. For the people of the Blasket, the art of poetry had imprinted itself so deeply on their minds that even their personal experiences tended to assume an artistic form.

Tomás has gone out for a stroll.

Today I turned my face towards a strip of land known as Spit of Seal Cove, a spot famous for its view, mostly of the north coast of the Island. I stopped there. I was in high spirits, and since it had been my habit for some time to take note of what I saw, that is what I now set out to do. . .

I was alone, enjoying the brilliant sunshine, with many thoughts passing through my mind, as I gazed at the scene that lay before me. . . After a while, still reclining on my side, I was roused by sounds of Gaelic as fine as I had ever heard, carried towards me on a gentle breeze. They were still some way off, and hidden from me by a shoulder of the hill; but I could distinguish the sound of their voices and the clarity of their words and the flavour of their speech. . . Then they came into full view, six of them, six grown girls, a perfect match in figure, face and dress. Anyone who did not know them would have sworn by the book that they were all from the same womb; and indeed he would not have been far wrong, because they all belonged to the same stock. The tune was so beautiful, and sung with such zest, as though by a single voice, and the girls themselves so lovely to look at, as they sang, that anyone with the true Gaelic spirit would have gladly spent a long summer's day listening to them without food or drink.

Allagar na hInise

As a poet himself, Tomás might have anticipated such an encounter, but he could hardly have expected six of them!

Muiris is on the train to Dublin. His two fellow-travellers are asleep. He too has been dozing, but is roused by the whistling of the train. He jumps up and puts his head out of the window.

The night at that hour had a lonesome look. It was bitterly cold. There was nothing to be heard but the duga-do-dug of the train and now and again the fairy music of the wind driving against the window panes. My thoughts were far away – as far as the Blasket.

I see the canoes out west of Carrig Vlach, and I hear the glug-glag of the ripples lapping against their sides.

I see some more of them close inshore at Yellow Island Beach, and still more back at Tail Rock, the nets at full stretch astern with sea-fire all round them.

I see the old crew – Seán Liam, Tadhg O'Shea, and Tomás O'Carney. There they are, chatting. Look how they clap their arms to keep warm!

I see the gulls hovering over the nets, and look how they swoop on the sea-fire as if it were mackerel!

I see a seal snorting at the end of the nets, and hear Tadhg O'Shea cast a curse at him: "Blindness and darkness on you – you won't leave us a fish alive in the nets tonight."

I hear the grating of the oars as they make for home without a single fish in the bottom of the boats.

Not a sound is to be heard but the lonesome murmur of ripples in and out of the rocks in the dead of night, a dog barking in the distance, and the whole village fast asleep.

Duga-go-dug, duga-go-dug! Then another whistle from the train. I shut my eyes tight, and soon the village appears in perfect likeness before my face; for, as the poet said long ago, "with the full power of my passion I strove to bring her before my eyes".

Fiche Blian ag Fás

This is an *aisling* in the making. Lulled by the rhythmical clatter of the train, Muiris imagines himself to be standing at Spit of Seal Cove, from which point he *sees* and *hears* all (note the repetition) until, closing his eyes, he beholds, not the fair maid of the folk-songs, not the Éire of the peasant poets, but the Island. Then, recalling a verse from O'Carolan, he realises that it is only a dream and wakes up.

It may be surmised that in earlier times, when the profession had been highly organised, the poet had conceived his *aislingí* in an actual state of trance, such as Muiris described – a state in which, in response to some rhythmical movement (in this case the clatter of the train), the poet withdraws from the external world into an illusory world of his own; then, having returned to reality, he shapes his experience into a poem. The listener's experience is less intense, but similar in kind. Poetry, it has been said, is "emotion recollected in tranquillity".

The emotional experience is personal and new, but the form in which it is recollected is traditional. Poetry is a union of the two. The poetical qualities inherent in Blasket speech are due to memories, conscious or unconscious, of the art of poetry as it had been practised over a period of more than a thousand years.

Towards the Novel?

There are two sides to the art of storytelling: the story itself, and the extraneous means by which the narrator enhances its effects – the inflections of the voice, the manual gestures, the laughter and the tears. The narrator is always something of an actor, who depends for his inspiration on the audience. He is quick to react to their response, and as they are carried away, so he too is moved to surpass himself, until all alike are spellbound.

This explains why folk-tales are so difficult to write down. A tape-recorder is no substitute for a living audience; nor can a visiting scholar, however sympathetic, take the place of a crowd of fellow villagers. As the art declines, the attendance falls off and the narration becomes perfunctory. It may well be that this was how the lyrics dropped out of the Irish tales.

To listen to Peig in her prime was an unforgettable experience:

> Big Peig – Peig Mhór – is one of the finest speakers on the Island; she has so clean and finished a style of speech that you can follow all the nicest articulations of the language on her lips without any effort; she is a natural orator with so keen a sense of the turn of phrase and the lilting appropriate to Irish that her words could be written down as they leave her lips, and they would have the effect of literature with no savour of the artificiality of composition. She is

wont to illustrate her talk with tales, long and short, which come in naturally along the flow of conversation, and lighten up all our discourse of the present with the wit and wisdom and folly and vivid incident of the past.

The Western Island

The art of storytelling is essentially oral; therefore, when it is committed to writing the most lively part of it is almost inevitably lost. One reason why the Homeric poems stand out in world literature as epic masterpieces lies in the circumstances in which they were written down. This, according to ancient tradition, was done by the minstrels themselves, who were fully literate and had maintained among themselves a centuries-old tradition of oral recitation. In the same way we may say of Tomás and Muiris, as compared with Peig, that they had the good fortune to be their own transcribers.

Before taking up his pen to write *The Islandman* Tomás had to be persuaded that the book would be worth reading. Only after Brian O'Kelly had read Gorky's *My Childhood* to him was he convinced that the story of a poor peasant fisherman might be of interest to the world at large. An even greater obstacle lay in the actual process – both the difficulty of mastering the new medium and the difficulty of conveying his most intimate thoughts and feelings to complete strangers, with whom he had no contact except through the medium of cold print. For Muiris the task was easier, because he had learned to write at an earlier age, but it was only after several failures that he learned to write as he talked.

Tomás was a man of few words. Like all the Islanders he enjoyed company, but with a certain detachment, sympathetic but gently ironical. Some of the entries in his journal recall the peasant scenes in Thomas Hardy's novels.

> I turned east towards the road. Glancing up to the village well, I saw a remarkable sight.
> Women and children were gathered there, some of the children dipping their heads in the water and washing them, then drying them with a towel, one after another till all were done, then off with them down to the school. Their mothers – those of them whose mothers were there – looked on without stirring hand or foot, leaving them to do that much for themselves.

Near the well is an outcrop of rock. Leaning against it
are as many grown men as there is room for. They are
waiting for others not yet ready to join them. They are
discussing laws. There is not a law under the sky but comes
under their scrutiny. Though half of them are unable to tell
A from B, they talk as if they knew as much about the law
as Aristotle.

When all are assembled, they move off up the road, driving some thirty asses before them. If one or two of them
have weak throats, others are audible three miles away.
Nothing can prevent the King or Seán Fada from making
their voices heard.

Since I still had my stick with me on account of my foot,
and since the sun looked as if it was about to scatter the
wretched clouds that have darkened the sky for so long, I
was in no hurry to get back, but sauntered on, with a glance
at each house and place as I passed.

A woman puts her head out of the door and sees a canoe
ready to leave for Dunquin. She lets out a yell that is heard
all over the village. Then her fat lump of a daughter puts
her head out too. "Mother Mary," cries the mother, "look
at the boat setting out for Dunquin, and your devil of a
father is not in it, though he knows we haven't had a grain
of flour in the house these three days, while that gallowsbird
sits chatting with the neighbours and the boat sails without
him. The devil, go and see if you can find him, and
whichever house he is in, may the roof fall on no head but
his!"

Allagar na hInise

Tomás was reticent by nature. His narrative style was incisive
and unemotional. In his books he seems to be feeling his way,
uncertain how much of himself to reveal. His marriage was
arranged for him. He tells us even less about his wife than Peig
tells us about her husband. His family life was clouded by adver-
sity but, apart from the death of his eldest son, drowned off the
White Strand, he passes over it in a couple of paragraphs:

Ten children were born to me, but they had no luck in life,
God help us! The first to be baptised was only seven or
eight years old when he fell from the cliffs and was killed.
After that they were no sooner come than gone. Two of

them died of the measles. Every disease that came our way carried off one or another. Donald was drowned trying to rescue the young lady off the White Strand. I had another fine lad, who was just beginning to bring in a return, but soon after he too was taken from me. All this bore very hard on the poor mother, and then she was taken. I was never blinded till then. May God not blind me!

An tOileánach

There was a proverb: "Tears shed are bitter, but not so bitter as tears unshed". Tomás's family was no exception. With no doctor and no district nurse, the rate of infant mortality was very high, and the hazards of cliff-climbing were an ever-present threat, no less than the perils of the sea.

The full impact of *The Islandman* is felt only in the final chapters. The author looks back over his life and the life of the community, both now drawing to a close:

I have written in detail about many events in our lives, so that there might be some record of them somewhere, and I have tried to describe the character of the people around me, so that they may be remembered after they are gone, for the likes of us will not be seen again.

An tOileánach

Again we are reminded of Hardy, who immortalised his fellow-villagers:

William Dewey, Tranter Reuben, Farmer Ledlow
　　late at plough,
Robert's kin, and John's, and Ned's,
And the Squire and Lady Susan, lie in Mellstock
　　churchyard now.
"Gone," I call them, "gone for good, that group
　　of local hearts and heads". . .

Whereas Tomás looks back on the past with a certain aloofness, Muiris throws himself into it. Writing about his childhood, he becomes a child again. He describes his responses to the world around him as he felt them at the time, and he brings his fellow Islanders, young and old, to life in the same way. This quality of immediacy, which we have already noticed in the story of Ventry Races, is derived from the folk-tale, and it is one of

Muiris's achievements as a writer that he has carried it over so successfully into the new medium.

The dialogue form is maintained throughout. Even the fireside tales are presented within a framework of incidental comments and asides. This gives us a story within a story as, for example, when the stranger is describing the six men he met in the enchanted castle:

> "As soon as they saw me, they stopped, put their hands under their arm-pits, and bowed their heads. And as sure as I am here tonight," said the stranger, striking his fist on my grandfather's knee, "I recognised every one of them, all of them dead for years before."
>
> A cold shiver ran up my spine.
>
> "Well, well," said my grandfather, "it's a wonder the soul did not fall out of you."
>
> "Indeed," said the stranger, "my courage was as good then as it is now, only I felt very queer when I recognised the six. I wanted to speak to them, but my tongue would not let me."
>
> "No wonder for you," said my grandfather.
>
> "He made a good stand," said my father, re-lighting his pipe.
>
> "Go on, stranger," said I, for I seemed to be seeing the six men with their heads bent down, and I did not want the story to be interrupted.
>
> *Fiche Blian ag Fás*

The story reaches our ears by two channels, so to speak: directly from the narrator, and indirectly through its effect on the listeners. This device – a story within a story – is as old as Homer. In the *Odyssey* the story of the hero's wanderings after the fall of Troy is told as a traveller's tale. This serves to reproduce an atmosphere of audience participation, which is so vital an element of the storyteller's art.

Finally, the Blasket writers were faced with the task of integrating their autobiographical tales into a comprehensive life-story. Here again Muiris achieved a notable success.

As Forster points out in his foreword, the reader of *Twenty Years A-Growing* is attracted by two features – the gaiety and the magic. The gaiety of youth and the magic of the old Gaelic world, the one blooming, the other in decay. These two opposing forces gather momentum as the story proceeds from the day of the races to the wedding day, from the first visit to the Inish to the last journey there, the little world of the Blasket opening out by degrees, until it is time to face the long road to Dublin. The story moves like a piece of music, revealing a sustained sense of artistic unity. This quality is lacking in the other books.

After this it might seem that Muiris had only to abandon the first person in order to produce a novel, but that step was never taken. The novel is a story of a new type. The oral and collective elements have been completely eliminated and the subject is the personal relations between individuals in modern society. All this lay beyond Muiris's experience.

The Generation Gap

Peig's outlook on life was medieval. She was so deeply involved with the old Gaelic world that she scarcely realised it was passing away. Life, as she saw it, is a journey through a vale of tears:

> There was nothing, it seemed to me, in the things of this world but poverty – this place full today and empty tomorrow. Those whom I had known in my youth had often had the stone in the sleeve for one another; they had been tough, fearless, strong-worded; but they all fell, they were all cleared out of the world. Those who had been there before them had met the same fate. God help us, where are their works today? Others are in their places without the least remembrance of them. All is folly, it seemed to me, save only the love of God.
>
> *Machnamh Seanmhná*

Tomás's outlook, too, was medieval, but he saw that the world was changing, and not, in his opinion, for the better. He considered that the old men he remembered from his youth were better men than those now growing up:

> They had no flour or butter or tea, and I believe they were better without, for one man of those days was better than three today.
>
> *Seanchas ón Oileán Tiar*

61

Old Owen agreed with Tomás:

"What used you to have?"

"Yellow meal, oatmeal, potatoes and fine fish from the sea, and they left their mark on the people. Little sickness or infection came to them. Arra, man, the way they are now, they wear shoes as soon as they can crawl, not to mention all the clothes they have on them, and for all that they are weak and will be. Would you believe it, it is many a day I left the house at sunrise, myself and Stephen Donlevy, Pad Mór and Seán O'Carney, for we were the crew of the one boat, dear God bless their souls, they are all on the way of truth now."

As he spoke, the tears fell from the old man, and he paused for a while as if to put from him the catch at his heart.

"Well," said he drawing a long sigh, "would you believe it, we would have nothing on leaving the house but five or six cold boiled potatoes, and we would not come home till the blackness and the blindness of the night? Where is the man who would stand up to such hardship today?

"There was no flour to be bought, no tea or sugar. We had our own food and our own clothes; the pick of the strand, the hunt of the hill, the fish of the sea and the wool of the sheep. The devil a bit there was to buy, Muiris, save tobacco, and you could get a bandle of that for threepence. So where was the spending?"

Fiche Blian ag Fás

What the old men complained of, therefore, was that the new generation preferred to buy what they needed rather than produce it with their own hands.

The young people were not convinced. Faced with permanent unemployment at home, they knew from relatives who had already "taken the long road" that jobs were to be had in the big cities overseas and so, suppressing all regrets for the past, they booked their passage from Cork.

The depopulation of the Great Blasket Island is not to be explained entirely by the failure of the fishing industry. The young people would have abandoned it even if the fishing had not failed. There was also a cultural factor. Within the space of a single generation their whole outlook on life had been transformed by literacy, which opened up a new world of commercialised mass entertainment.

If you argued with the old people that this or that detail in the folk-tales could not be true, they would reply that at the time in question Ireland was "under magic", and there was no more to be said. They had many superstitions in which they believed with varying degrees of certainty. Tomás records a dialogue between Seán Fada and his wife Mainy:

> "I heard the cuckoo today, upon my soul," says Seán, "whatever it may signify. I wonder, Mainy, if anyone else has heard it?"
>
> "I have no knowledge of it."
>
> "You are not so blind to other people's business."
>
> "Why all this worry about it? Why is it that, whenever something untoward occurs, you let it get under your skin like nobody else in the village?"
>
> "But, my little woman, don't they say it's not a good sign for a man to hear it. And I heard it clearly."
>
> "That depends on where it is coming from. Did you hear it behind you? If so, that's not a good sign. Many people have heard it in front of them – that's nothing serious."
>
> "Yerra, the devil, didn't I hear it both in front and behind? Read me that riddle, little woman. It was calling in front of me when I was facing uphill, and it was calling behind me when I turned round towards the sea. So, you see, little woman, it is hard for a man to protect himself, if there's any harm in it."
>
> *Allagar na hInise*

There were also differences between the two generations in matters of religious doctrine. The young people were no less devout than their elders, but they were more critical.

At the top of the village, close to the well, stood a house, named in jest the Parliament House, where the old men used to meet in the evenings to discuss world affairs. It was also frequented by passers-by on their way to or from the well. Máire Guiheen writes:

> One evening I went to the well to fetch a bucket of water. Not far away was the house of Máire na Dálach. I put down my bucket and went in. Máire was there with Mártan, Muiris, Eibhlís and Seán. They were having a weighty dis-

cussion. Seated in her corner, Máire was telling them that they were destined to marry whatever boy or girl the One Above had appointed for them.

"Amn't I telling you that it is so?" said she to Mártan.

"Well, girls," said he to us, "it seems you have only to sit on the stool in the corner there, and the man appointed by the One Above, the God of glory, will come into the corner and fetch you out."

"He will so," said Máire, "I have seen them come. Something will happen to bring them together. You will find that my words are true."

"Then why do you spend so much time making a match for this boy and that girl, if it has all been settled beforehand so surely as you think?"

"Amn't I telling you again that it is so, only God ordered help."

"Yes, and he also ordered that you yourself must help yourself."

I remember another evening when a bright young lad said to Máire:

"If heaven is up above, isn't it from there that all bad things come – rain, snow, thunder and lightning?"

"What is that you are saying?" she replied. "Rain is not a bad thing; it moistens the earth for growth. Thunder and lightning put fear into our hearts and make us think of God. The sun and moon, which give us light and warmth, are in the sky and so too are the stars, which are a delight to look up at on a frosty night, sparkling like jewels. Now what do you say, my boy? Understand yourself before you speak."

"Well," says my boy, "if hell and the big fellow are down below, isn't it from there that the grass grows, and our food, and pretty flowers, and all good things?"

"Never mind where hell and the big fellow may be, but beware of his tricks and ways, and put God's cross between you and him for as long as you may live."

An tOileán a Bhí

The old people made up in eloquence what they lacked in logic.

The Mythical Background

To the question, did the young people believe in the folk-tales, there is no simple answer. Their attitude was ambiguous. They were inclined to reject the stories, but without abandoning their belief in the supernatural. There were many superstitions which they would dismiss without hesitation as old wives' tales, yet they would be careful to observe them in practice. They continued to believe in spirits. In general, they seem to have been feeling their way towards a distinction between the world of everyday life, from which magic is excluded, and the world of fantasy, in which the imagination has free play. Here again a comparison between Tomás and Muiris is instructive.

Tomás records the events of his life just as they occurred, without conscious selection and without embellishment. This does not mean that his account of the facts is purely objective for, as we have seen, it bears the stamp of a strong personality. Muiris's method is different. What he gives us is not primarily a factual account at all but an artist's impression of certain selected episodes. This does not mean that he misrepresents the facts; on the contrary, he is a keen and accurate observer, even of the smallest details; but he has recast his material in retrospect so as to present the essentials of each situation in a concrete and concentrated form. This method may convey more than a factual record, just as an artist's portrait may reveal more than a photograph. Both methods contain a subjective element, without which there can be no art, but Muiris's is the more consciously artistic.

Tomás sets out on his first seal hunt. He is the youngest member of the crew and is proud to be doing a man's work:

> Well, we put out the four oars – stout, long-lasting, broad of blade and sweetly sounding – as the Fenians used to do in the old tales, and with all speed on a straight course made our way to the cave we had decided on for the hunt.
>
> *An tOileánach*

Muiris and two companions are rowing across the Great Sound when they sight a whale bearing down on them:

> We were in great danger – out in the middle of the Great Sound, a couple of miles from land, and that savage, ravenous, keen-eyed, long-toothed monster up beside us, the way it had only to turn its head and swallow us up.
>
> *Fiche Blian ag Fás*

Here the Fianna are not mentioned by name, but the epithets make the allusion clear. Such encounters were not infrequent and could be very dangerous, so there was real cause for fear. If the beast was so ferocious, they had good reason to liken themselves to the heroes of old. On the other hand, they were not giving chase to the monster; it was chasing them. This allusion is not without a touch of humour.

The same is true of our next example. Tomás Owen Vaun is fighting Cosey, with Muiris at his back exhorting him in the name of his ancestors. This is how the Fianna used to fight their duels, each of the combatants with his supporters behind him taunting him and goading him into action. Muiris notices the parallel, and when the fight is over, he says to Tomás:

> "Do you know what I was thinking, when I saw you and the other fellow fighting, especially on Ventry Strand? I was thinking of the duel between Dáire Donn and the King of France long ago; for Dáire Donn was a tall, lanky fellow and the King of France a sturdy little block of a lad like yourself."
>
> "By God," said Tomás, rubbing his hands with glee, "we were like enough to them."
>
> *Fiche Blian ag Fás*

It is not to be inferred that Muiris was making fun of the heroic tales. Such comparisons came to his mind readily because they were so close to his heart. Here is another comparison where he is quite serious:

> Discontented though I had been ever since I went into the Depot, a cloud was now rising from my heart, when I saw the view – the earth white with snow, the foliage on the trees bending under the burden they were carrying, the wind whistling shrilly through the woods. Hundreds of crows were flying from tree to tree, and before long I saw a couple of deer galloping away from the terrible host that was bearing down on them. Musha, did I not think at once of the Fianna – of Oscar and Conán Maol and Goll Mac Morna!
>
> *Fiche Blian ag Fás*

What puts him in mind of the Fianna? Down in Ventry, on the edge of the bay, there was a wood called Móin Mhór, and the old people said that in ancient times Fionn and his companions used to hunt there.[1]

Of all the Fenian tales the one the Islanders loved best was the story of Oisín in the Land of the Young. That country, they said, lay far out to sea to the west of Inish Vickillaun, the most pleasant and mysterious of the Blaskets. The old people said that it had remained "under magic" right down to their own day, and in proof of this they quoted a tune called "The Fairies' Air" which they said had been overheard from the fairies there about a hundred years before.

Muiris pays three visits to the Inish. It is on the third of these that he decides reluctantly to stay in Ireland and not to emigrate. Looking out over the sea, he sees a vision of the Land of the Young:

> The sky was cloudless, the sea calm, sea-birds and land-birds singing sweetly. The sight before my eyes set me thinking. I looked west to the edge of the sky and I seemed to see clearly the Land of the Young – many-coloured flowers in the gardens, fine bright houses sparkling in the sunshine; stately, comely, fair-headed maidens walking through the meadows and gathering flowers. Oh, if only Niamh of the Golden Hair would come here now, thought I, I would

gladly go with her across the waves.

Fiche Blian ag Fás

As he gazes again at the horizon, the Land of the Young merges into America; the land of youth into the land of gold.

It seemed to me now that the New Island (America) lay before me with its fine streets and great big houses, some of them so tall that they scratched the sky, gold and silver out on the ditches and nothing to do but to gather it. I see the boys and girls who were once my companions walking the street, laughing brightly and well contented.

Fiche Blian ag Fás

If Oisín had stayed in the Land of the Young he would have become immortal, but, overcome with homesickness, he returned to Ireland, and no sooner had he set foot on his native soil than he became a decrepit old man, unrecognised and unrespected. All the youth overseas and only the aged at home – was not this the fate of the Blasket people? The same thought occurs again in the conversation on the quayside in Cork:

I looked round. He was standing by my side – a bent old man, well worn with the hardship of the world. He had a knitted cap on his head, a clay pipe in his mouth, a grey beard under his chin, and boots up to his knees. I saw he was a man of the sea. "You don't mind my asking, is it beyond you are going?"
"It is not, but near it."
"Your girl that has gone before you, perhaps?"
"Musha, the cause of my sorrow is every boy and girl who were once in my company. They have all turned their backs on this quay, and I am like Oisín left alone after the Fianna."

Fiche Blian ag Fás

These passages show that the heroic tales were being transformed in the writer's mind into a realm of the imagination. They are used in such a way as to cast an afterglow from the old Gaelic world over the story of his own life.

Here too there is a lesson to be learned from the Blasket books. The stream of traditional Gaelic poetry has drained away along with the language, but it has not quite ceased to flow. It might still be revived if the riches of Gaelic mythology were channelled into it. Of course the Gaelic poet, like all poets, must have something significant to say to the contemporary world, but he must do more than imitate what other poets are saying in other languages. He must produce poetry that is as Gaelic in style and spirit as theirs is English or French or Greek, and this can best be done if he makes creative use of the traditional forms, and treats the ancient myths as a quarry of images and ideas. That is what has been done by the poets of modern Greece, whose work is now known in translation all over the world.

Fuit Ilium

Let us return to Homer.

In the *Iliad* the Greeks are at war. It is an age in which rival chiefs enriched themselves by means of cattle raids and plundering expeditions, their prestige resting directly on their individual fighting capacity. Such conditions had once prevailed in Ireland and were remembered in the heroic tales.

The scene of the *Odyssey* is laid in Ithaca, a rugged island in the far west. Its ruler, Odysseus, who is one of the less wealthy chiefs, is not ashamed to work with his hands. Besides being a soldier and a huntsman, he is a sea-captain, carpenter and stonemason, and can do a day's mowing in the fields as well as any man. He possesses household slaves, and these are his property, but his relations with them are personal and direct. He belongs to an age in which social inequalities have not yet created a cultural cleavage between the palace and the peasant's hut.

By the time these poems were completed in their final form the conditions described in them had been transformed. Where there had been only villages there were now populous cities, flourishing centres of commerce and the arts. The Homeric poets looked back with regret to the "heroic" virtues of the past, and their nostalgia is reflected in the poems themselves.

Nestor, the oldest of the chiefs who fought at Troy, is complaining that the others will not listen to his advice:

I have consorted with better men than you, and they heeded my advice. I do not see now, nor shall I ever see, the likes of Peirithoos and Dryas, Kaineus and Exodios and Polyphemos, who were the strongest men on earth and fought against the strongest. There is no man living today who would be a match for them.

These are the very words of Tomás.

The island of Ithaca had little to offer besides mountain pasture – "It is a rough place," says Odysseus, "but a fine nurse of men." One might say the same of the Blasket Island.

Odysseus returned home in disguise and found shelter with his swineherd, a gentle, gracious peasant extraordinarily like Old Owen. Listening to Old Owen at the fireplace, as he told of the hardships endured by Pierce Ferriter in his struggle against the English, one could not but recall this swineherd weeping for his master who had perished, he believed, at Troy. Notwithstanding all the differences of time and place, the personal relationship is the same.

The comparison is not new. Professor Luce has drawn attention to Homeric qualities in the life of the Blasket Islands, and Professor Delargy has spoken of the "heroic age" which lasted till our own day on the western coasts of Ireland and Scotland. If Odysseus was a hero, so was Tomás, and Old Owen and their contemporaries commemorated in these books. This is what Seán O'Crohan has to say in his own book about an old man who had just died in the Parish of Mórach:

> Diarmaid Donnacha O'Begley died today in Dingle Hospital at the age of eighty. He must have been the tallest man in the district. He was seven feet in height and well-built in proportion. He was an accomplished Gaelic speaker, but, as he used to say himself, "Neither Gaelic nor English ever put a morsel on my plate". He was a one-cow farmer and a fisherman too – as good a fisherman as ever sat on the thwart of a canoe. He spent his whole life in the jaws of the waves, never knowing whether he would come back safe or leave his corpse to the crabs. That had to be done when Diarmaid was earning his livelihood. The jetty from which he went fishing was neither safe nor sound, and when he was caught in a storm he would often put in at Baile na nGall. Nothing pleased him better, because it gave him an

excuse for a pint, which he never refused.
A hero laid low. The peace of heaven to his soul!

Lá Dár Saol

We should not regret the passing of that world. No doubt, the Blasket was a delightful place in summer. As they said themselves, "You would not leave it for any other place short of Paradise of the Bright Saints".[1] But it was no paradise in winter nor in times of scarcity and sickness. One has only to recall what was involved in fetching a doctor or a priest.

> Next morning someone came to the door to say that the old man had been complaining for days and asking for the priest. No one who was able to go could refuse such a call – a three-mile journey out to the mainland and back with the priest, then out again with the priest and back – twelve miles in all of sea and wind and tides.
>
> *Lá Dár Saol*

No wonder the Islanders were a little critical of those friends whose enchantment with the Blasket way of life led them to overlook the lack of essential services which they took for granted in their own lives:

> Visitors coming in and going out of our house talking and talking and they on their holidays and they at home having comfortable homes and no worry during winter or summer would never believe the misfortune on this island, no school nor comfort, no road to success, no fishing, not five hundred of mackerel was caught last summer when it cost £3 a hundred, no lobsters last summer, very very scarce, hard times, everything so dear and so far away. Surely people could not live on air or sunshine. No, not at all.
>
> *Letters from the Great Blasket*

We must also remember that a similar economic upheaval had taken place in other European countries and brought widespread suffering, though nothing so calamitous as the Irish famine. This was followed in England by a period of rapid growth, with a demand for labour in both industry and agriculture; and as labour became more mobile the old rural culture, based on the village community, was destroyed. According to Hardy, the disappearance of the Dorset ballads dated from the building of the railway, which brought in a flood of popular magazines from London. After noting the general rise in the standard of living, which he had seen in his lifetime, he writes:

> But the changes at which we must all rejoice have brought other changes which are not so attractive. The labourers have become more and more migratory – the younger families in especial, who enjoy nothing so much as fresh scenery and new experience. The consequences are curious and unexpected. For one thing, village tradition – that vast mass of unwritten folk lore, local chronicles, local topography and nomenclature – is absolutely sinking, has nearly sunk, into eternal oblivion.
>
> *Life of Thomas Hardy*

With the growth of modern industry it was inevitable that the old relations, together with the traditions that cemented them, should be dissolved. Civilisation has always advanced through conflict, bringing losses as well as gains, but the losses may be made good in the future if we can learn to draw inspiration from the past.

Town And Country

Hardy defines the difference between town and country in the light of his own experience:

> London appears not to *see* itself. Each individual is conscious of *himself* but nobody is conscious of themselves collectively, except perhaps some poor gaper who stands around with a half idiotic aspect. There is no consciousness here of where anything comes from or where it goes to – only that it is *present*. . . The fiendish precision or mechanism of town life is what makes it so intolerable to the sick and infirm.
>
> *Life of Thomas Hardy*

With this definition in mind let us return to Muiris's journey to Dublin.

Born and bred in a closely-knit community based on kinship and co-operation, he is now caught up in a machine so vast and complicated as to be incomprehensible to its individual members, whose relations with one another are motivated by competition and self-interest. It is not often that we have the opportunity of seeing our world through the eyes of an unsophisticated observer, who is himself looking at it for the first time.

The author presents his story in the guise of a folk-tale. Guided by the leprechaun whom he has met on the hillside, he goes out into the world to seek his fortune, and he encounters many miracles and

marvels, which are to us no more than everyday realities. All
this is light-hearted comedy. He is a little sentimental at times
but this is offset by his readiness to laugh at himself. Beneath
the laughter there lie some penetrating observations of urban life.

After leaving Ballyferriter he stops and looks around him,
afraid that he may have taken the wrong turning.

> Soon I saw an old man in tatters coming down towards
> me from the hill, an old yellow pipe between his teeth, a
> couple of cows before him. He was making towards me and
> calling Sho amach! sho amach! to the cows.
>
> When he came down to the road, I greeted him. He
> returned my greeting in fine Irish.
>
> "Listen here, my good man, is this the right road for
> Dingle?"
>
> "It appears you are a stranger in this place," said he.
>
> "I am, good sir."
>
> "Oh, have no fear. Do you see those telegraph poles?
> Follow them and they will lead you into the town."
>
> "A thousand thanks to you."
>
> "You are welcome," said he, shaking my hand and going
> down the road to the west.
>
> *Fiche Blian ag Fás*

This chance encounter is brief but warm, and sealed by the
parting handshake.

A little further on he meets another wayfarer.

> I was making my way eagerly forward, when I saw
> coming towards me a swell of a gentleman with a chain
> round his belly, a hard hat on his head, and an umbrella
> in his hand. I greeted him.
>
> "Is that Dingle to the east?" said I.
>
> He stopped and looked at me, looked to the east, then
> looked at me again. "Have you any English?" said he.
>
> "I have," said I in English, "but I want to know how far
> I am from Dingle still?"
>
> "Oh yes, yes," said he, taking out a little handkerchief
> and wiping his brow, for I think he was sweating from the
> walk, "that's it over there among the trees."
>
> "Thank you very much," said I going east.
>
> *Fiche Blian ag Fás*

Here we have the same exchange of question and answer, but no personal contact. These two thumb-nail sketches convey almost to the point of caricature the contrast between the poor peasant and the respectable burgher.

Next day, seated in a railway compartment for the first time, he looks around:

> I was soon deep in thought, looking out through the window at the fields and valleys which were darting by, and looking in at the people, wondering who they were, where they had come from, or what business had taken them from home to send them rushing through the middle of Ireland.
>
> *Fiche Blian ag Fás*

A few minutes later he learns from the ticket inspector that he is on the wrong train.

> The train was whistling from time to time and with every whistle my anxiety was growing. Through the windows of the corridor I could see now and then noble gentlemen talking together and laughing merrily. I wonder, said I to myself, if you knew there was a poor traveller like myself gone astray, would you give him any help? I suppose you would not; for, as the old saying goes, the fat does not notice the lean.
>
> *Fiche Blian ag Fás*

On arrival in Cork he fights off the ticket touts who take him for an emigrant, and makes his way into the city, where he meets a blind beggar:

> What did I see but a man standing up in a corner with a very strange appearance on him – a big stick in his hand, which he moved from side to side as if he were feeling the place with it, his face turned upwards, some kind of board hanging down his breast, and he muttering to himself. Now and then he would take off his cap and make the sign of the cross. People in plenty were passing by, but they took no notice of him. By my baptism, said I, you are a strange one, and it is a great wonder you get no heed from the people that are passing by. After a while I walked over to him. I could see now what was written on the board: Have a heart and help the blind! Oh, thought I, woe to him who would

complain! O God, give help to this poor blind man here! In the name of God, said I, whatever I will do without money, I will spare a small sum to you. I put my hand in my pocket and gave him a shilling.

Fiche Blian ag Fás

Down by the quays he meets the old fisherman.

"I tell you I was well off once, a fisherman with a motor-boat owned by myself and my four sons. But my sharp sorrow! the fishing went under foot, and my heart was sorely smitten a year ago on the spot where the two of us are standing now, when my four sons said farewell and turned their backs on me out through the harbour. Ah, it is little I thought," cried he mournfully, "ye would leave me alone as I am."

Hunger was oppressing me by this time, for I had been fasting since two o'clock. So I said goodbye to the old man, who was gazing sorrowfully out, as if he were talking to the great sea.

Fiche Blian ag Fás

These two "poor gapers" made a deep impression on the Blasket boy, because in them he saw some of his most cherished values – help for the needy and respect for one's parents – flouted in a society which claimed to be more civilised than his own.

What pleased him most when he left Dublin was not that he had made the grade as a policeman but that he was going back to his own people:

I went down and walked as far as the gate. Children were playing up and down the road, calling to one another in sweet, fluent Irish. I heard the sound of footsteps approaching. He was within four yards of me before I saw him, because he was wearing a suit of bauneens of the same colour as the ground.

"God bless you," said the old man.

"God and Mary bless you," said I.

"A fine night," said he again.

"It is so, God be praised."

He passed by. Before long another was approaching.

"God bless you."

"God and Mary bless you."

"A fine night."

"It is a beautiful night, praise be to God on high."

I stayed awhile, listening to the sound of the wind in the trees and watching the glitter of the moonlight on the sea. Then I turned on my heel and went in.

Fiche Blian ag Fás

Muiris never reconciled himself to the task of enforcing the law against these people. He came from a community which had lived without the intervention of the police and with only moral sanctions:

It was a sort of self-government. If you committed an offence or did something wrong, the people would not be content to let it pass. You had always to keep to the straight path, otherwise the people would intervene and correct you.

Leoithne Aniar

Buying and Selling

How are we to evaluate the culture enshrined in these books in relation to our own?

Many visitors returning from the Blasket to Dingle and Tralee must have felt as Synge did on returning to Galway from the Aran Islands:

> I have come out of a hotel full of tourists and commercial travellers to stroll along the edge of Galway Bay and look out in the direction of the islands. The sort of yearning I feel towards those lonely rocks is indescribably acute. This town, that is usually so full of wild human interest, seems in my present mood a tawdry medley of all that is crudest in modern life. The nullity of the rich and the squalor of the poor give me the same pang of wondering disgust; yet the islands are fading already, and I can hardly realise that the smell of the seaweed and the drone of the Atlantic are still moving around them.
>
> *The Aran Islands*

At other times his mood was different:

> On some days I feel that this island is a perfect home and resting-place; on other days I feel that I am a waif among the people. I can feel more with them than they can feel

with me, and, while I wander among them, they like me
sometimes, and laugh at me sometimes, yet never know
what I am doing.

The Aran Islands

He is disenchanted with his own society, yet cannot give it up.
He is drawn towards the Islands, yet something holds him back.
It may be that this contradiction contains the answer to our
question.

It has already been noted that the decay of folk traditions was
brought about by the growth of literacy, which is regarded by
many archaeologists as the hallmark of civilisation. It should be
seen, however, as only one of several interrelated factors, which
in their totality constitute the transition from primitive to
civilised society. Writing was invented to serve the needs of trade.
Trade presupposes the exchange of goods between persons
engaged in different kinds of labour. These divisions of labour
led to others – between mental and manual labour, town and
country, rich and poor. All these relations were mediated by
money. Without money there could have been no markets or
fairs, no accumulation of wealth or leisure, no flowering of the
arts and sciences, such as was seen in ancient Greece and again
later in Western Europe – in a word, none of the cultural achievements of modern civilisation.

Money began to circulate in Greece as far back as the seventh
century BC and came into general use throughout the Roman
Empire, but after the collapse of the Empire there was a setback.
Long-distance trade was at a standstill. The revival that followed
marked the beginning of the capitalist era in Western Europe.
There were, however, many outlying or secluded communities
whose economic relations remained for a long time confined to
the local market. The Blasket was one of these.

Thus, when we describe the Blasket culture as medieval, we
mean that it was relatively untouched by the advance of modern
industrial society. But, like everything else, civilisation has a
double aspect. If the Blasket people were unaffected by its posi-
tive aspect, they had no part in its negative aspect either. What
is the negative aspect of civilisation?

The circulation of money dissolved the old village communities, based on co-operation and mutual aid, and merged
them into larger units in which people confronted one another

as buyer and seller, with money as the only bond between them. In the words of an ancient Greek poet, "man is money"; that is to say, a man is worth the money in his pocket. There was nothing that could not be bought or sold. "Gold," wrote Columbus, "constitutes treasure, and he who possesses it has all the needs in this world as well as the means to rescue souls from purgatory and restore them to the enjoyment of paradise." Peig Sayers had a quatrain expressing the same idea from the opposite point of view:

> The man without riches is not recognised at the wedding;
> The man without riches speaks and his voice is ignored;
> The man without riches is unable to order or spend;
> The man without riches is a prey to the woes of the world.
>
> *Machnamh Seanmhná*

The Blasket men went to Dingle as sellers and buyers. They sold their surplus products at market and bought consumer goods in the shops. They were under pressure to sell, even at a low price, because they needed the money, and they were under pressure to buy, even at a high price, because they needed the goods. There was no love lost between them and the shopkeepers. They complained of overcharging, the shopkeepers of unpaid bills. When they faced each other across the counter, they did so in an antagonistic relationship quite different from that which prevailed among themselves.

Tomás describes how he bought a pair of braces:

> I went into a clothes shop belonging to a woman who was a relative of mine.
>
> "Arra, God bless your life from the west," said she.
>
> "Long may you live, my good woman," I replied.
>
> If I called her "good woman", it was for good manners only, because I knew from previous acquaintance that she was not to be commended. She was putting questions to me, enquiring about this person and that, waiting for the moment when I would ask for what had brought me there. Now and then I would put my hand to my pocket, and her eyes would sparkle in her head, with a glance round the shop and then back to me.
>
> "Show me some braces," I said. I would have kept her even longer in suspense, only I was in a hurry to get back

to Diarmaid.

She lost no time in laying out a bundle of them, because her hands were rusty with the lack of business. "These are a shilling a pair," she said. "They are foreign-made."

I took up one pair to see what they were made of. "I would have needed a dozen of these to hold up my breeches yesterday," I said, "when I was lifting the pig out of the cart. Give me the best you have. If they are foreign-made, keep them till the foreigners come and ask for them."

A woman who had just come into the shop burst out laughing when she heard my cheeky answer. The shop-keeper went red in the face. She put the foreign goods back and brought out a bundle of the old sort. I picked out one pair, handed her a shilling, and departed.

An tOileánach

The encounter begins with an exchange of those reciprocal salutations which are such a gracious feature of the Irish language. In general, they were more than a formality – rather, a conscious affirmation of the speakers' humanity in the sight of God. But on the present occasion they are only a pretence. Forgetting their kinship, the two range themselves against each other as buyer and seller. It is no surprise, therefore, to learn from Seán O'Crohan that in this antagonistic relationship some of the Islanders sometimes broke the rules.[1]

After the collapse of the fishing the Islanders had nothing left to sell but their labour. The remittances they sent home from America were a portion of their wages. As the eastward flow of money increased, so did the westward flow of young men and women. The movement was organised on a family basis:

The eldest girl was usually the first to go. She would spend a year or two at work in Dingle or somewhere, saving up for the fare. She would be keen to go; her relatives would help her and fares were quite cheap in those days. I believe you could get from Cobh to New York for six pounds. Having obtained employment over there, and seeing that her brothers at home were unable to find work, . . . she sent them the fare, one by one, as soon as she could; and when they in their turn had got jobs there, they would have to repay their sister out of their earnings. Meanwhile the next sister was sending the fare to another of them.

That is what destroyed the youth and vigour of the Islanders. They went to America.

Leoithne Aniar

To these exiles America offered an escape from the poverty of their home life, but only on condition that they surrendered their cultural values. Some of them paid the price without regret, others only with a lifelong sense of loss. For a few the price was too heavy, and they came home.

The Blasket that will be

The Blasket people had used money for several generations, but only as a means of exchange – selling in order to buy. They had no experience of buying in order to sell – that is, investing in some commodity in order to sell it at a profit. They had monetary relations with the landlords and their agents and with the jobbers and shopkeepers of Dingle, and they received remittances from overseas. These external dealings had little influence on the relations that existed among themselves. No money circulated in the Island. They were bound to one another by close ties of blood and marriage, all residing within a stone's throw of each other, all engaged in the same occupations and faced with the same dangers at sea. They were a community of kinsfolk. They had their quarrels, of course, but seldom carried them beyond a war of words. When a stranger came to the Island they offered him the same hospitality, no matter who he might be. They did not think the less of him if he was poor nor the more of him if he was rich. If they wished to praise him, they said he was "both noble and humble". They were not easily deceived by pretentiousness or conceit. The virtue they admired the most was what they called *mórchroí*, "greatness of heart", that is, a spirit of humanity uninhibited by calculations of self-interest. They had little formal education and no political understanding, but were well versed in their own ancestral lore, which was perfectly adapted to their way of life. It was a narrow life, but their knowledge of it was profound. It was a simple culture, but free from the rapacity and vulgarity that is destroying our own.

Are we to conclude, then, that these cultural values are destined to disappear along with the communities that nurtured them?

The industrial revolution that began two centuries ago is still continuing on an ever-increasing scale and raising the productivity of labour to a level previously undreamt of. It is now technically possible to satisfy all the basic needs of the world's population, provided that each man's share of the wealth produced is proportionate to his labour.

These changes have involved a social upheaval even vaster and more disruptive than the mass migrations from Europe to North America. The peasants who flocked from Europe to the United States in the last century could at least look forward to employment there. That hope is denied to the millions of displaced peasants herded together in the shanty towns of Latin America and Africa. In English cities there are back-streets populated by immigrants from the Punjab and Bengal, who had enjoyed at home a cultural life comparable in all respects with that of the Blasket Island. This paradox of poverty in the midst of plenty has been the law of a monetary economy ever since men first went to market, but in our day it has become catastrophic. The free play of market forces must be brought under control if our civilisation is to be saved from self-destruction, and that can only be done by the deprived and the dispossessed. When they take their future into their own hands they will cast off their backwardness and, by releasing new forces, material and spiritual, raise civilisation to a higher level.

Photographs of
The Blaskets, 1923–34

1. Tomás O'Crohan and his son Seán.

2. Maidhc O'Shea ("White").

3. Pádraig O'Daly (Paddy na hInise).

4. Seán O'Crohan, Eibhlís O'Sullivan, Tomás O'Crohan and Muiris O'Sullivan.

5. Muiris O'Sullivan and his grandfather Eoghan "Daddo" O'Sullivan.

6. The house of Pádraig O'Keane, An Rí (the King). The figure sitting down outside is the King himself.

7. Seán O'Crohan, Eibhlín O'Sullivan, Hanna Filí Kearney, Mícheál O'Guiheen (Maidhc File), Muiris O'Sullivan, unidentified boy.

8. Máire Pheats Taim Kearney and Siobhán Keane (June Bhofar).

9. Children on the White Strand Eibhlín Guiheen, Lís Guiheen, Hanna Filí Kearney, Cáit Sheáisí Kearney, Nora Keane, Cáit Mhuiris Eoin Bhán O'Connor, Lís Mhicil O'Sullivan, unidentified girl, unidentified girl, Máire Mhicil O'Sullivan (back). The boy on the extreme right is Maidhc O'Sullivan; third from the right, at the back, is Mícheál O'Guiheen.

10. Máire Bean Uí Catháin stands outside the door of her house.

11. Children at Tobar a'Puncán, "The Yank's Well" beside the "Dáil" or "Parliament House". Hanna Pheats Taim Kearney, Margaret Keane (Peig Bhofar), Máiréad Keane, Máire Guiheen, unidentified girl, Nellie Pheig Sayers Guiheen.

12. A view of the mainland from the Island.

13. The north side of the Island, looking south-west towards An Chró. Tobar Builteóra and Cuas Faill Bheag are the two prominent inlets; the tower, of the Napoleonic era, was destroyed by lightning in 1934.

14. George Thomson.

15. The Island from Dunquin harbour.

16. Inish Tooskert from the Island, with Oileán Buí in the foreground.

17. Back from the market, at the top of the quay. The King's son, Seán O'Cro-han, is carrying his youngest child. In the background is the mainland.

8. Daddo and George Thomson.

19. Professor Carl Von Sydow leaves the Island.

Appendix
"The Sorrowful Cliff"

Note

The following episode was omitted – mistakenly, as I now think – from the English edition of *Twenty Years A-Growing*. It continues on from the day – recounted in the chapter "Pierce's Cave" – which Muiris spent with his grandfather.

One afternoon some time later my grandfather and I were sitting beside the fire, waiting for my father who was out fishing pollock.

"Musha, daddo," said I, to start him talking, "I dare say it's many a fish you ever caught."

"There's no doubt that I caught many a good fish one time in my life," said he, looking into the fire. "But do you know what was the best fishing ground here long ago?"

"What was it?" said I.

"The Sorrowful Cliff," said he. "As for cod, pollock, ling, hake, white eel, bream, it is there they were; boats would be coming from the north and boats from the south, boats from the east and boats from the west. And did you ever hear why it is called the Sorrowful Cliff?" said he again, bending down and putting another spark in his pipe.

"The Devil I heard," said I.

"I will tell you now the reason," said he, pulling at the pipe again and sending smoke all over the house until he had it softened to his satisfaction. Then he spoke again. "Now," said he, "you know where Ballymore in Ventry parish is?"

"I do," said I.

"There was a man living there up to eighty years ago whose name was Seán O'Moran, a small farmer on the edge of the harbour and a small fisherman too. There were no motor cars or trains in those days, nor any thought of them, and therefore when a man was able to have a firkin of butter, he would go to Cork with the firkin on his horse's saddle. And so early one fine morning he set off for Cork with the firkin up on his horse's saddle, and before long he was passing a little roadside hamlet when he noticed a crowd of people outside a little thatched cottage, a coffin slung across two chairs and one woman keening bitterly over it. Seán stopped to let the funeral go by. No one was stirring.

"By the Book, said Seán to himself, I don't know if this is the custom here to leave the corpse like that so long, but I will soon find the answer to that question. He leapt from his horse and went into the crowd, and, said he to the first man he met – 'what is the reason for their standing here, or what is the purpose of it?'

"'Musha, comrade,' said the stranger, 'that is a poor widow who had nothing in the world but her one son, and there he is now lying in the coffin. As for the purpose of their standing, I will now explain it to you. You know that every landlord is demanding five pounds for the patch of land to bury a corpse in, and therefore the landlord will not allow the widow to bury her son without paying that sum of money, but that is something she cannot do.' Seán went up to the widow and addressed her.

"'May I ask what is the cause of your sorrow?' She lifted her head and looked up.

"'O musha, my good sir,' said she, 'it is my fill of the crosses of the world. My only son on the way of truth, and I unable to bury him in God's earth without paying five pounds. And I have not a red penny.'

"'Don't mind that,' said Seán, putting his hand in his pocket and handing the five pounds to her, and off he goes back to his horse."

"Musha, daddo," said I, "what a wonderful spirit he had!"

"See he did indeed," said my grandfather, bending down and putting a spark in his pipe again.

"I'm telling you," said I again, "that Seán got blessings from the old woman when he was leaving."

"Yes indeed, and he deserved them," said my grandfather, crossing his knees. "Well, to make a short story of it, at the end of the following harvest the fishermen of the barony were preparing themselves for the season, and as I told you already, the best fishing ground at that time was the Sorrowful Cliff. It is there they were coming from Crooked Creek, from Dingle, from Ventry, from Dunquin, from Iveragh, from the Rodanna, from White Mouth, from Doonin, as far as Leitriúch to the north and as far as Kenmare to the south. From every harbour boats were coming to the Sorrowful Cliff one evening when the sea was dead calm.

"Seán himself was a fine fisherman, and he had a boat of his own, but it happened that evening that he was a man short, and the three who were in the same boat with him were at his house, discussing where they would find a man for the night, when a strapping young boy, a stranger, came in the door. He greeted those who were there, and they greeted him. He stood between the doorposts.

"'I would greatly like to know,' said he, 'if you are in need of a serving boy for a year.'

"'By God, I am, especially at this fishing season just now we are short of a man.'

"'If so,' said the stranger, 'I am able to manage boats, and if you like I will go with you tonight.'

"'Very good,' said Seán, 'let us be moving forward so in the name of God.' Off they go and it wasn't long before they were passing through Dingle Bay back westwards towards the Sorrowful Cliff. It was a wonderfully fine night – not a puff from out of the sky, but the sky was breathless like plate glass, the morning star gleaming beautifully between them and Mount Eagle. Sixty boats with their nets stretched out in the sea peacefully, and a man had no work to do, just floating, a snatch of a song being thrown up here and there, and now and again the whistle of a curlew as it passed across the sky.

"The stranger was in Seán's boat without a word. This surprised them that a traveller like him should be without any news at all. If so, it is soon that he stood up in the stern of the boat.

"'Well, Seán O'Moran,' said he, and every member of the crew gave an ear to him. 'I came to you this evening and I made a bargain with you for one year, and take heed that I have already been paid, and therefore take my advice now, and draw in your nets as fast as ever you can, because it never blew from the skies as badly as it will blow tonight.' Seán laughed, and the three others too.

"'It is no matter for laughter, Seán,' said the stranger, 'and take heed and I will give proof to you. Do you remember a year ago today when you went to Cork with a firkin of butter that you gave five pounds to my mother in order to put me in God's earth? I came tonight in order to give you a return. Make all haste now, and if you have any relatives, or people you wish to save, call them home without delay.' With these words he leapt into the sea and was never seen again. Seán and his crew were struck with trembling, hand and foot, for they knew he was from the other world.

"'For God's sake,' said Seán, 'draw the nets in as quick as you can, because he is a man of good counsel, and what he says is true.'"

"By my baptism, daddo," said I, "I dare say they were terrified."

"Indeed," said my grandfather, "they were terrified and anxious, but not for the dead man but for the storm that was coming."

"I suppose so," said I, "go on with your story."

"Where did I stop?" said he.

"You stopped," said I, "where Seán told his crew to draw their nets in."

"Yes indeed," said my grandfather. "Off they went, drawing in the nets for all they were worth," said my grandfather. "And when they'd done that, off they all went, and set about calling to the other boats, but my sorrow, they were all laughing at Seán. Why should they not be? The finest night that had ever come, and to say that night would blow! And with herring leaping in the nets, to draw the nets in! When they took no notice of Seán, he hoisted up his sails and went off through the Dirty Sound eastwards. They were no further than half way when the sky darkened and storm clouds gathered in the south-east, with a broken sea between them and Iveragh. It was blowing and blowing, ever and ever, until they had to lower the sails. They were edging their way forward past Little Cove. It is there that two halves were made of the mast.

"'God help us,' said Seán, 'we have made land, but those who are out are out, and those who are in are in.' Will you believe that sixty widows were made that night, not to mention all the young men?"

"It was a great slaughter," said I, and I noticed the tears falling from the old man with the fit of sorrow which came over him. Well, said I in my own mind, there's no limit to the old man's kindheartedness.

"Whenever I look at that place, daddo," said I, "it seems to me very sorrowful."

"It is so," said he, "and no wonder, because I think, Maurice, with all the curses that were cast at it, the fish have avoided it ever since."

G.T.
completed 18 January 1987

Addendum

My father noted that a similar incident, with slightly different details, was related by Peig Sayers and Tomás O'Crohan. He calculated the year of the disaster to have been during the mid-1830s, although he said that no record of a storm in that area existed. I commented on some general points of similarity with Irish folk-tales in Seán O'Sullivan's collection, and in particular with No 24, "The Man Who Was Rescued From Hell" (pp. 151-64). That was the last but one text I read to my father, the final one being his introduction to Kostís Palamás, *The Twelve Lays of the Gipsy*

Margaret Alexiou

Drawings by

Muiris O'Sullivan

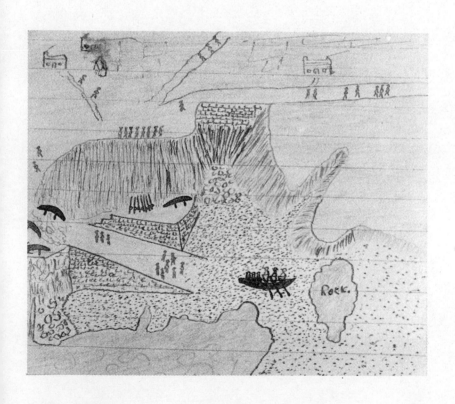

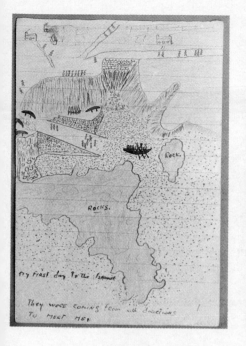

ROCKS.

ROCKS.

My FIRST day TO THE ISLAND

They were coming from all directions
To MEET MEY

1

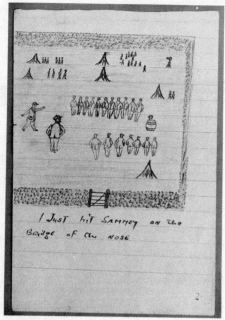

I JUST hit SAMMEY on the
BRIDGE of the NOSE

2

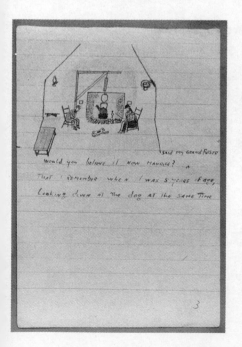

SAID MY GRANDFATHER

Would you believe it NOW MAURICE?
THAT I remember when I was 5 years of age,
Looking down at the dog AT the same Time

3

DUNQUIN PIER

SEA

COCK

I GOT A TERRIBLE FRIGHT
AS I Though the CANOE WAS A
BIG BEETLE COMING Towards me.

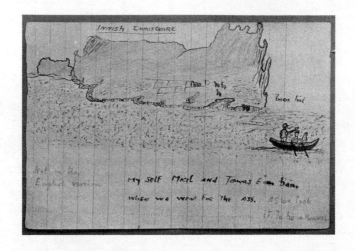

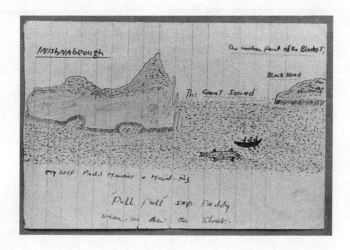

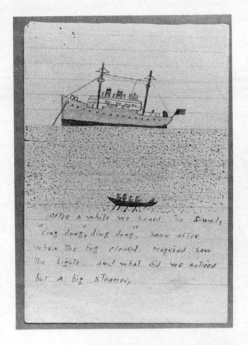

AFTER a while WE heard The Sounds
"ding dong", ding dong, soon after
when The Fog cleared. Maghead saw
The Lights, and what did we noticed
but A big Steamer,

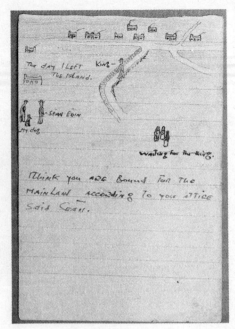

The day I LeFT King—
The Island.

— Sean Eoin

My dog

Waiting for the King.

I think you are Bound For The
MAINLAND according to your ATTIRE
Said Sean.

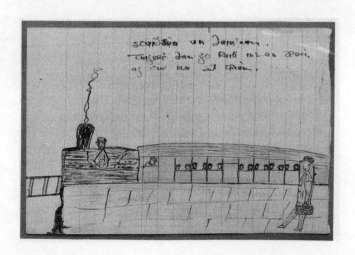

Stiúrsún un Jarnéan.
Tuigeac dam go Raib mé an Doctor
ag cur me ail Triáin.

George Thomson

A Memoir

1

The 27th August 1923 was a day of high drama in Ireland – the first General Election under the Free State constitution was being held. Among the 150 inhabitants of the Great Blasket, three miles off the Kerry coast, the excitement was no less than elsewhere. The arrival of a young Englishman that day to sojourn on the Island caused no small stir too. They had a good English friend already, Yorkshireman Robin Flower.

Máire Guiheen recalls the day:[1]

> I went down to the landing place when the currach was approaching. My father was coming in with two other men. I was only a slip of a schoolgirl at the time and have forgotten who they were. Out of the currach stepped a courteous, slightly built young man with dark hair and a pleasant smile. He wore a rain-cloak and I made a wonder of this, for I had never seen a man or a boy with one. I gave him a thousand welcomes and was delighted that he understood me, that he had some Irish.

In *Twenty Years A-Growing* Muiris O'Sullivan describes his own encounter with the stranger that fine sunny day:

> He was now only forty yards away, a man neither too tall nor too short, with knee-breeches and a shoulder cloak, his head bare and a shock of dark brown hair gathered straight back on it. I was growing afraid. There was not his like in the Island. Where had he come from and he approaching me now from the top of the hill in the darkening of the day? I leant my back against the bank of the ditch. I drew out my pipe and lit it. Then I turned my gaze out to the south-east, thinking no doubt he would pass me by on his way,

so that I could take his measure and say I had seen a leprechaun.

I heard a voice behind me. "God save you," it said.

I looked round. He was smiling.

"God and Mary save you, noble person," said I.

He sat down on a stone beside me and drew out a box of cigarettes. "Will you have one?" said he in English.

"I will not, thank you," said I in Irish.

I was taking his measure well as we spoke and he looking out to Iveragh. We both remained silent for a long time. Then he tried to say something in Irish, but failed. So he turned again to English.

"What do you call that place over there?" said he in a very hard accent.

"They call it Valentia Island," said I in English.

"And how would you say that in Irish?"

I told him. He took from his pocket a little book and a pencil and wrote down quickly what I had said. Faith, my lad, said I to myself, this is not the first time you wrote Irish anyway. When he had finished I spoke to him.

"Where are you from, may I ask?"

"Repeat that, please."

"Where are you from?" I repeated very slowly.

He bent his head for a moment, muttering the words under his teeth. Then he answered in English. "I am from London, and I came to the Blasket today," said he with a laugh. (The laugh of an Englishman, said I to myself, isn't it often I was told to beware of it!)

He asked my name. I told him.

"Mine is George Thomson," said he in Irish.

"I'm thinking you have Irish too," said I.

"A little," said he with another laugh.

It was growing dark and we moved east towards the village. He was questioning me about this word and that word in Irish, and I giving him their meaning. When we came to the top of the boreen: "Where are you staying?" said I.

He stopped for a moment to think: "I am in the house of Michael Guiheen. Is that right?"

"It is," said I, "and as I said before, you will soon improve in the language."

Máire takes up the story of his arrival at her house:

> We showed him his room and then asked him to sit in to
> the table. He had his tea and afterwards my mother
> suggested that he should sit in the corner by the fire. He
> did so and was soon pointing to the potrack and asking
> what it was called in Irish. I told him. He continued asking
> the name for this and that. My father was sitting on the
> settle answering questions too.

By the end of the first day Thomson had a stock of Blasket
words. As Muiris O'Sullivan said:

> There is no doubt but youth has great ability. George and
> I spent the next six weeks walking together on strand, hill,
> and mountain, and after spending that time in my company
> he had fluent Irish. If everyone in Ireland were as eager as
> he for the language, the people of old Ireland would be
> Gaels again without much delay.

Eibhlín O'Sullivan, sister of Muiris, kept a diary in which, on
27 August, she commented on voting day in Dunquin. Her first
reference to Thomson is on 30 August: "I have not seen the
young Englishman since he came to the village". But on 2 September she wrote:

> We had high sport since morning, for many strangers came
> in. We were sitting above by the roadside along with the
> English boy and another lad – I think he is from Tipperary:
> the Englishman is very friendly altogether.

Within a week of his arrival George Thomson is at home among
the young Islanders – watching the "strangers" coming in! The
other Englishman, Robin Flower, was a friend of the older
generation, of Tomás O'Crohan and Peig Sayers.

Eibhlín was confined to the house for three weeks with tooth-
ache but another diarist, Mícheál O'Guiheen, son of Peig Sayers,
recorded on 7 September:

> I am going down to the harbour now along with George,
> an English boy who is lodging with Mike Léan Guiheen,
> the King's son-in-law. He is a friendly lad and has a camera,
> taking pictures with it of the King and everyone around.

Tomás O'Crohan was the first Islander to take to the pen. He started with a journal and extracts from it were published in 1928 under the title *Allagar na hInise*; it was the first Blasket book. Tomás encouraged the younger generation, Eibhlín and Mícheál, to keep journals too. Mícheál, who was already composing poetry, became, like Muiris, a close friend of Thomson's; the three young men were of similar age.

On 22 September Eibhlín records:

> Last night was my first time going out for three weeks. . . Máire Sheáin and I went to the top of the village to George. When we arrived he was in the house looking at several photographs spread out on the table. He asked if we would like to see them. We said we would and what was the very first one he handed us but a picture of myself, little Eibhlís and two or three others. Then we examined all the snapshots which were very good. When we finished with them we played little games and had high sport.

Máire Guiheen recalls that Thomson not only joined in the games with which the young Islanders were familiar but that, among other things, he introduced chess to the Blasket.

He was taking more photos on 29 September, as Eibhlín writes:

> I put on Muiris's cap with its peak turned backwards and I held a book in my hand. He asked me to stop laughing but, my sorrow, I never laughed more than at that moment when I thought of the cap on my head.

Tír na nÓg had to come to an end, however, and Thomson left the Blasket the next day. Eibhlín again:

> George has left us today and we are rather lonesome after him. Two girls went away too and we miss them very much, for there are few girls here now and I suppose those few will not stay. People are like birds; as soon as they are ready to leave the nest they take flight leaving the father and mother behind. Few people have ever left this place without feeling lonesome and George was near to tears, saying that he would much prefer to be here than in London. The Island is like a ship sinking with everyone trying to make their escape.

Mícheál O'Guiheen recorded:

> Poor George is leaving today and he is very lonesome. We

are at the top of the landing place now ready to go out. Máire Keane and Siobhán O'Guiheen are leaving too. The Island will have few girls now for most of them have gone already.

The omens were not good but Thomson had arrived in time to sit at the feet of "the Master", Tomás O'Crohan, and to spend rainy days listening to Peig Sayers telling stories. And, although he had spent less than six weeks among the Islanders, his departure is seen as that of an emigrant! He had come to the most remote outpost of western civilisation in search of spoken Irish and found that he had rediscovered Homer's Ithaca, the island of Odysseus, "A rugged place, but a good nurse of men".[2] His sojourn there would be momentous for Muiris O'Sullivan and the Blasket, for Ireland and the whole future life and work of George Thomson himself.

Back in London he did not forget his friends. On 12 October Mícheál recorded that he had received a letter, a present of a book and his photograph. A letter came to Eibhlín too on the same day along with the photograph in which she was wearing Muiris's cap. He returned to the Blasket regularly during the next decade and in the intervals kept up correspondence with the Islanders, including Tomás O'Crohan, who sent him poems he had written. As for Muiris O'Sullivan, he became the closest friend Thomson would ever know.

2

George Derwent Thomson, one of a family of five, was born in West Dulwich, London, on 19 August 1903. His father was a chartered accountant. His mother and her father were ardent champions of Irish Independence; he was an Ulsterman of Orange stock who, rebelling against family tradition, embraced nationalism and emigrated to London. From them Thomson inherited an early interest in Ireland. He was a pupil at Dulwich College from 1916 to 1922. The Black and Tan campaign of terror drew him more towards Ireland and after school on Monday afternoons he would tear off his Officers' Training Corps uniform and go up to London to attend classes run by the Gaelic League. There he took the first steps in the language of which he was to become so consummate a master.

In 1922 he was awarded a scholarship to King's College, Cambridge. Instead of Classics he would have read Celtic Languages if they had been available. However, he was determined to continue with his Irish and, in the rooms of J. T. Sheppard, the teacher who taught him "the right method of approach to the study of Greek poetical technique", he had a chance meeting with Arthur Waley, the Chinese and Oriental scholar from the British Museum. When Waley learned that Thomson intended going to the Gaeltacht he advised him to consult Robin Flower who was working on the catalogue of Irish manuscripts in the museum's collection. Flower advised Thomson to go to the Blasket, where the two men subsequently met from time to time. Flower, a distinguished medievalist, was deeply versed in the culture of the Blasket and Thomson acknowledged his debt to him.

Thomson took First Class Honours in Parts I and II of the Classical Tripos and was awarded the prestigious Craven Scholarship in 1926. This enabled him to spend a year at Trinity College Dublin, working on his first book *Greek Lyric Metre*. While he was there Muiris O'Sullivan arrived to join the Garda Síochána.

In the summer of 1926 Thomson had been back on the Blasket. Muiris describes the last visit they made together to Inish Vickillaun. His sisters Máire and Eibhlín and his brother Seán had already gone to America:

> He looked at me between the two eyes and after a while he spoke gravely:
> "Well, now, there is no one but the two of us on this lonely island and so I hope you will put courage in my heart."
> "I will do it if it is in my power. Let you put the question."
> I knew well what was the question he had to put to me.
> "The question is, have you cast America out of your head?"
> I got up without speaking a word. It was often before

that George was urging me not to go across to America but to stay in Ireland and enter the Civic Guard. But there was the reluctance of the world on me to do as he said, and I was trying to put off the matter always. But the last day was come now and both of us knew that if I did not agree with him that day I would be gathered away before the summer was come again.

Muiris accepted the advice of his friend. The latter left the Island the next day and Muiris says:

I noticed now a thing I had never seen before. I did not see the smile on George's mouth. It was enough. He had his fill of sorrow and my own heart blackened likewise.

3

During the same year Thomson made his first visit to Greece. Just as the Blasket had re-invoked Homer's Ithaca for him, so in Ithaca, while listening to the old women talking, he thought he was back on the Blasket. He had left the rest of his party to continue with their tour of the ancient monuments while he made his own way to that island.

He would say later:

Like every student, I was deeply impressed when I found myself standing under the shadow of the Parthenon. But this feeling did not last. It gave way to an oppressive doubt: "There was only one Hellas, and she is gone and will not come again".

Before making the journey I had got hold of Thumb's *Handbook of the Modern Greek Vernacular* and picked up a smattering of the spoken language, just enough to maintain a precarious conversation. Looking back after all these years, I find that what I learnt from Thumb's *Handbook* has meant more to me than all the monuments of antiquity.

His debt to the "experience of Irish peasant poetry" which he discovered on the Blasket he acknowledged in *Greek Lyric Metre,* as he would do again and again. Part of the inspiration for that book came from a passage in one of Yeats's essays:

> The relation between formal music and speech will yet become the subject of science, not less than the occasion of artistic discovery. I suggest that we will discover in this relation a very early stage in the development of music, with its own great beauty, and that those who love lyric poetry but cannot tell one tune from another repeat a state of mind which created music and yet was incapable of the emotional abstraction which delights in patterns of sound separated from words.

The systematic study of the common origins of poetry and music would occupy Thomson for many long years. It was a study that occupied Gerard Manly Hopkins also who, during his last years as Professor of Greek at University College Dublin, was writing a book on Greek lyric metre, but the manuscript was lost. In his *Gerard Manly Hopkins* W. H. Gardner wrote:

> The work which Hopkins failed to complete has been carried out, in part at least, in such a book as Thomson's *Greek Lyric Metre,* an exposition which explains admirably many of those aspects of the Greek "individual metres" which bear the most striking resemblance to the rhythms of Hopkins.

In a review of Thomson's book J. T. Sheppard commented: "This is a masterpiece of lucid exposition". Even Thomson's style of writing had been influenced by his Blasket experience. He would become a polymath but never a pedant and, however profound the subject matter, would always write with a euphonious lucidity uncommon in learned work. So deep had been the effect of the Island's oral culture upon him that he would never commit anything to print without first reciting it aloud to hear how it sounded.

4

Muiris O'Sullivan arrived in Dublin in March 1927 and Thomson was waiting for him at the station. They then went to stay for a week with Moya Llewelyn Davies in her early Georgian mansion at Furry Park, Raheny. Moya was the sole surviving daughter of James O'Connor, Nationalist MP for Wicklow, whose wife and six children had all died of cockle poisoning at Blackrock, County Dublin, in June 1890. She married Compton Llewelyn Davies, a distinguished civil servant in London, and was a prominent champion of the Independence movement and of women's rights on Liberal Party platforms. It is said that she bought the mansion at Furry Park as a wedding present for Michael Collins and that it was after his death she went to live there herself.

Muiris described the house as "a big castle, a magnificent lamp alight above the door, the walls covered in ivy, up to twenty windows in it, big and broad" and Moya as "a girl, young, handsome, brightly laughing. I saw she was of the flower of nobility. She gave me a thousand welcomes."

After Muiris's period of training at the Depot in Phoenix Park he was posted to Indreabhán in County Galway. He was soon at home in the Connemara Gaeltacht which, he said, reminded him of the Island. Police work he would never grow to like, however, especially having to hunt out poteen makers. In his *From the Irish Shore* Captain Denis Ireland tells of Muiris:

> Apparently, after a recent case in which he was giving evidence, the judge, who was plainly a man of taste, descended from his dais, shook him warmly by the hand, and the pair of them were seen strolling up and down the main street of the village, exchanging comments on literature.

George Thomson returned to Cambridge and from 1927 to 1931 he was a Fellow of King's College. While holding his Fellowships he returned to Trinity College Dublin during 1929 to work on his edition of the *Prometheus Bound* of Aeschylus, the poet on whom he would become an authority.

5

It was the policy of University College Galway to introduce teaching through the medium of Irish and two classical lectureships were established on that basis in 1931. George Thomson applied for one of them. Academic achievement merited an interview, so the story goes, but it was the flow of Blasket Irish that astonished the interviewers. He got the post.

The appointment caused astonishment in other quarters too. Cambridge wanted to keep him, especially as a teacher of Greek lyric metre, and E. R. Dodds, Professor of Greek at Birmingham, wrote that he had "left Cambridge to bury his talents in Galway as a lecturer at a small and remote university college". This was in Dodds's memoir of Stephen MacKenna, the famous translator of Plotinus, whose *Journal and Letters* he edited. An entry in the journal reads: "Henceforth it is to be first Ireland and second politics and then – third but very dear – Greek". Thomson might have written this himself if he had kept a journal in later years.

The Professor of Greek at University College Dublin, Michael Tierney, went even further than Dodds when he wrote that it was foolish to attempt to teach Greek through the medium of a patois. And people still remembered the remarks of another Greek scholar, Professor Mahaffy of Trinity College Dublin, who claimed that Irish had no use in any practical system of education, though it was sometimes useful to a man fishing or shooting in the west!

Thomson, however, far from burying his talents in Galway, would make a unique contribution to the Gaelic revival as an editor and translator of Greek classics for the Department of Education, and as editor and translator also of the Gaelic and world classic *Fiche Blian ag Fás* or *Twenty Years A-Growing* by Muiris O'Sullivan.

6

In 1929 Muiris had complained to his friend that he found the winters long when there was little to do outside, so Thomson urged him to write a book following the example of *An tOileánach* by Tomás O'Crohan. Muiris set to work with the aim of "passing the time for the old women of the Blasket and giving them a laugh, for great was the fondness and love I had for them when I would visit them during the long winter nights".

Tomás wrote in powerful and restrained narrative of a heroic world that was passing away. The currach could not compete with giant trawlers which came scouring the sea-beds after the First World War and the young were attracted in a steady stream to the bright lights of Springfield, Massachusetts, the next parish west. Muiris on the other hand, with imaginative recreation and lyrical recall, sang of boyhood wonders at the edge of the western world.

Fate had brought the two friends together again and Muiris would bring batches of his manuscript in to Galway. The work was finished in 1932 and comprised 500 pages of closely written script, too long for publication. On the other hand, Thomson reminded the author of incidents he had forgotten. Finally the editing began. In this capacity Thomson was "like a man carding wool or winnowing oats from chaff. The only help I gave the author was to guide him towards adapting for publication the craft he had learnt from his grandfather as a child by the fire".

They were not always in agreement about the sections to be omitted. One such was "The Sorrowful Cliff". In the end they decided that it should appear in the Irish version but be omitted from the translation. This Thomson later regretted and, just before he died, he dictated a beautiful rendering of it for this book. Thomson relates:

> After I had typed the second version of the manuscript I went through it again from beginning to end with the author to see if I had made any mistake. Then I gave the typescript to An Gúm (Government Publications). They agreed to publish it on two conditions: the story in Chapter Five, about the two boys getting drunk, would have to be omitted for fear of setting a bad example to the young, and the book should not be translated into English. We thought the first

condition nonsense, nor were we satisfied with the second either because I had already translated it into English with help from Moya Llewelyn Davies, and it had been accepted by Chatto and Windus. We therefore submitted it to another publisher who did accept it.

This publisher was the Talbot Press and its reader was Pádraig Sugrue, "An Seabhac", editor of Tomás O'Crohan's *Island Cross-Talk* and *The Islandman*. The book came out in 1933, the same year as the English version, the first translation of a Blasket book to appear, and both were reprinted before the year was out. Thomson had rendered it directly into English and Moya Llewelyn Davies had re-written it in "the Irish dialect of English as being nearest to our original, and in this respect we are following the example of Synge".

Seán Ó Faoláin claimed that "it is for Irishmen the most exciting thing that has happened within a hundred years. It is the first piece of literature in Irish since the scattering of the poets in the eighteenth century". W. B. Yeats thought the English version "perfect of its kind, it has elegance". In an Introductory Note E. M. Forster had called it "the egg of a sea-bird – lovely, perfect, and laid this very morning".

In the same year also the Viking Press published it in America and it became a best seller on both sides of the Atlantic. It has appeared in the Golden Library, the Queen's Classics, as a Penguin, and in the World's Classics Series of Oxford University Press. Currently it is an Oxford paperback. It has been read again and again on Radio Éireann and the BBC. Projects for a film of the book have been mooted from time to time, for one of which Dylan Thomas wrote a script. However, a film of it has yet to be made. It was translated from English into other languages, including French and German. The French version *Vingt ans de jeunesse* was by Raymond Queneau and Elizabeth Aman's title for the German version, *Inselheimat*, was adopted by Thomson for the present book.

Professor D. A. Binchey wrote in *Studies*, December 1934:

> Apart from native speakers, there are few Irishmen who have achieved Mr Thomson's command of the spoken language. His edition is a model of accuracy, in eloquent contrast to the slovenliness of many native editors.

7

Thomson had demonstrated his command of the spoken language in *Breith Báis ar Eagnuidhe,* his translation of the *Apologia,* the *Crito* and the *Phaedo* of Plato, published in 1929. It is the language of Plato the gods speak on Olympus, we are told. Besides being a poet himself, Plato, in his dialogues, was still close to the oral poetry out of which Homer had come. In the Blasket Island oral poetry had been passed on from generation to generation. It also moulded not only their storytelling but everyday conversation through which poetry was, in Thomson's happy phrase, "constantly bubbling up". It is doubtful if English translations have ever quite captured Plato's limpid style, with its humour and its vivid vignettes of life in the fifth century BC. However, Thomson, with remarkable rapport, had rendered him into the language of Tomás O'Crohan, Peig Sayers and Muiris O'Sullivan.

One person who appreciated this book was Stephen Mac-Kenna: "I have read it and will read it again". He had been introduced, says Dodds, to George Thomson:

> a youthful Fellow of King's College, Cambridge, who shared his dual passion for Greek literature and for the Gaelic speech. Thomson became a great favourite, and figures frequently in the letters of these years, now as "Dante" or "Geoffrey Chaucer", now as *Fear na féasóige,* "the bearded one" (in reference to the beard which learned men should by tradition possess). MacKenna and he cherished in common the dream of fertilising the revived Gaelic culture from the same sources which at the Renaissance had given new life to the literature of France and England.

The two men, who also shared a love of modern Greek, had been introduced to each other by Liam Ó Rinn, author of an Irish book on MacKenna, and translator of *Poems in Prose* by Turgenev and *The Stars in their Courses* by Sir James Jeans. He acknowledged the ready and generous help of George Thomson with both of these works.

In 1932 Thomson, aware of "the great need for text books in Irish", brought out the *Alcestis* of Euripedes and next year the *Prometheus Bound* of Aeschylus, both with long introductions. The latter was an Irish version of the English edition on which he had been working for over five years. In the preface to the *Alcestis* he says:

> So far as technical terms are concerned, I believe it is fortunate that Irish has so few, especially in the realm of literature. If a term is wanting, the explanation should be given in a straightforward manner and with simple language which would benefit both teacher and pupil alike; a plethora of terms makes it too easy for us to disguise lack of knowledge with pedantry.

He translated other Greek works such as Homer's *Odyssey* and circulated them in typescript among students. Nor were his translations only from the Greek; for the Gaelic journal *Humanitas* he translated sonnets by Shakespeare. With Professor Osborn Bergin he translated the *Book of Common Prayer* for use in the Church of Ireland and for performance by Taibhdhearc na Gaillimhe he translated *Everyman*. He was much involved in the work of this Gaelic theatre and hoped to bring plays into the Gaeltacht too.

His hopes did not stop there. In Britain the practice of taking the benefits of university teaching to the public outside its walls was well established. Thomson wanted to start extra-mural classes along the same lines in the Gaeltacht. He wrote in Irish in *The Star*:

> Let us focus on Dunquin for example. There is an old ruin in the parish called Mór's House; Piaras Ferriter's name is well known in the district; and the men regularly go out fishing for mackerel. So, let us give a lecture there about Mór's House, when it was built according to the scholars, how it was built and why; this would arouse interest in prehistory. Let us give another lecture on Piaras Ferriter, on the poems he composed and the story of his life; this would arouse interest in history and literature.
>
> We could lecture on the life of the mackerel, how it spawned, every aspect of its habits and ways under the sea, thus leading to biology. We could explain how it is bought and sold in the towns which takes us to economics. We could deal with the weather and pass on to meteorology and astronomy. We could explain how beer is made and that leads to chemistry.

If we began in this way, dealing with matters that concern the lives of the people closely, there is no doubt that we would be able to arouse interest in the origins of things; for there are not many to be found more eager to follow up questions like these than the Gael from the west; all the signs are that lectures in the Gaeltacht would succeed, if only a start were made.

Thomson finished a short history of Greek philosophy himself for this purpose in 1932, *Tosnú na Feallsúnachta*. However, a start was not made. Thomson explains:

The Irish climate is not suitable for lectures in the open air. You need a hall. An Irish village has only one hall, the school. And the manager of the school is the parish priest. I had not proceeded far with my arrangements when it was made plain to me that there was not a priest throughout the length and breadth of Connemara who would dream of permitting his school to be used for anything so subversive as a university extension lecture in Irish or any other medium; nor was there any support forthcoming from the National University or the Ministry of Education to induce a change of mind. So that was that.

In 1934 the two friends parted again. George Thomson left Galway to resume his Fellowship at Cambridge and Muiris O'Sullivan left the Gardaí. After the success of his first book, Muiris hoped to make a living by writing. He married Cáit Keane of Carraroe in Connemara where they settled. They had two children; Eoin, actor, writer and broadcaster, and Máirín, who became a nurse. Muiris returned to the Gardaí in 1950 and in that year he was drowned while bathing.

8

During his first year back at Cambridge George Thomson married Katharine, daughter of Dr Hugh Fraser Stewart, Dean of Chapel at Trinity College, Cambridge, and of Jessie Stewart, pupil and biographer of the great Greek scholar and authority on religious origins, Jane Harrison. Katharine had attended Thomson's lectures on Greek lyric metre and had also taken First Class Honours in the Classical Tripos. Her main passion, however, was for music, which she studied in Germany. There were two daughters of the marriage; Elisabeth, now a teacher in Birmingham, and Margaret, who is Professor of Modern Greek at Harvard University.

England was in the grip of depression with hunger marchers passing through Cambridge, while fascism menaced Europe. In 1935 Thomson took the next big step in his life when he joined the Communist Party of Great Britain. It was not an unusual step for university people during that period; for many, communism would become "the god that failed". Thomson, however, would make a unique contribution to Marxism and remain an unwavering Marxist-Leninist all his days.

E. R. Dodds left Birmingham University to replace Gilbert Murray as Regius Professor of Greek at Oxford and early in 1937 Thomson succeeded Dodds, becoming the second person to hold the Chair of Greek at Birmingham, where he would remain. The Vice-Chancellor there told him that a classical education was the best antidote to communism! Thomson preferred to be at Birmingham which, he said, was the real world, while Cambridge with its elitism was "like a monastery garden". It was the year in which Christopher Caudwell died fighting in Spain, a young Marxist writer whose work Thomson would do much to foster. Both at Cambridge and in Birmingham Thomson was active on the Spanish Aid Committee.

His edition of the *Oresteia* of Aeschylus in 1938 marked him out as one of the great Greek scholars of the age. It was dedicated to Muiris O'Sullivan. The Professor of Greek at Trinity College Dublin, W.B. Stanford, said of it after discussing other well known editions: "Professor Thomson's book (771 pages in all) is outstanding among the editions of any century".[3] In the accompanying translation of the *Oresteia* into English verse, he captured the robust rhythms of the poet, using blank verse for the dialogues and following the metres of the original plays closely in the lyric passages. These were the translations chosen for the American Laurel Classical Drama series.

In Birmingham, as at Galway, Thomson would be a pioneer. Over a period of years he introduced Modern Greek as a normal part of the classical curriculum. This incurred the wrath of the conservative classicists who, with their colonial outlook, dismissed spoken Greek as a peasant patois. However, he had the able assistance of Dr Nicholas Bachtin, a Russian poet and linguist who left Cambridge in 1938 to join him. Together they worked out a new method for teaching Greek, both for students fresh to the language and those who had been taught it at school. They discovered that the easiest and quickest way was to study it scientifically, by means of historic linguistics instead of descriptive grammar. The value of this method was proved with ex-Servicemen after the war. In his *Greek Language,* published in 1960, Thomson explains:

> It is strange that so many classical scholars visiting Greece to refresh themselves at the fount of Hellenism should spend all their time contemplating the material remains of antiquity without realising that the object of their quest still flows from the lips of the people. The relation between Ancient and Modern (spoken) Greek is so close that they are treated by all the authorities, not as two languages, like Latin and Italian, but as one. The difference between Modern Greek and Homer is estimated to be no greater than the difference between Modern English and *Piers Plowman,* though there is a span of twenty-eight centuries in the one case and only six in the other. Hence, an English student reading Euripides with no knowledge of Modern Greek is at the same disadvantage as a foreign student reading Chaucer with no knowledge of Modern English. No foreign student of English would be so misguided as to cut himself off from the living source, and the student who approaches Greek in this way develops a creative activity which is real, not artificial, and finds that the ancient language springs to life.

The book was dedicated to the memory of Bachtin who died in 1950 and who, he said, "taught me to place my knowledge of the language on a scientific basis. With him I learnt Greek all over again." Thomson was never less than generous in acknowledgements to colleagues and predecessors.

After Bachtin's death the work continued and in 1964 lectureships in Byzantine and Modern Greek were established. Modern Greek became equal in status to any other subject. It received a big boost when the Ministry of Defence, wanting Greek-speaking interpreters for NATO, found that Birmingham was the only university which could supply their needs. Postgraduate studies were established and many students form Birmingham are now teaching Greek all over the world, including in Greece itself.

9

George Thomson had been studying the Marxist classics with the same intensity as he studied the ancient classics and, in 1941, the epoch-making *Aeschylus and Athens* appeared, a Marxist study of the social origins of drama: Aeschylus interpreted against the background of the evolution of Greek society from the tribe to the state. And in the preface, after paying tribute to such works as L. H. Morgan's *Ancient Society*, a book which James Connolly had championed, he wrote:

> I must also mention a special debt to my friends the peasant fishermen of the Blasket Island in West Kerry, who taught me, among many other things that could not have been learnt from books, what it is like to live in a pre-capitalist society. It is true that nominally they fall within the orbit of the capitalist system, because they are liable for rent, but most of them refuse to pay it; and in general their traditions, especially their poetry, date from a time when social relations were profoundly different from those in which I have been brought up.

In 1956 came *Marxism and Poetry*, perhaps his best known book.

It has been translated into many languages, including Arabic, Japanese and Chinese. My own copy was published in New Delhi, price One Rupee. He begins with his experience on the Blasket where "poetry has nothing to do with books at all". He tells about the Island poet Seán O'Donlevy and then says, "To some extent they were all poets". He gives "an example – one out of many".

> One evening, strolling through this village, perched high up over the Atlantic, I came to the village well. There I met a friend of mine, an old peasant woman. She had just filled her buckets and stood looking out over the sea. Her husband was dead, and her seven sons had all been "gathered away", as she expressed it, to Springfield, Massachusetts. A few days before a letter had arrived from one of them, urging her to follow them, so that she could end her days in comfort, and promising to send the passage money if only she would agree. All this she told me in detail, and described her life – the trudge to the turf stack in the hills, the loss of her hens, the dark, smoky cabin; then she spoke of America as she imagined it to be – an Eldorado where you could pick up gold on the pavements, and the railway journey to Cork, the trans-Atlantic crossing, and her longing that her bones might rest in Irish soil. As she spoke, she grew excited, her language became more fluent, more highly coloured, rhythmical, melodious, and her body swayed in a dreamy, cradle-like accompaniment. Then she picked up her buckets with a laugh, wished me goodnight, and went home.
>
> This unpremeditated outburst from an illiterate old woman with no artistic pretensions had all the characteristics of poetry. It was inspired.

Read aloud, this passage is itself poetry. George Thomson had caught the excitement from the old Blasket woman. He had discovered the key to Homer:

> The conversation of those ragged peasants. . . electrified me. It was as though Homer had come alive. Its vitality was inexhaustible, yet it was rhythmical, alliterative, formal, artificial, always on the point of bursting into poetry. . . One day it was announced that a woman in the village had

given birth to a child. As my informant expressed it, *Tá sé tarraigthe aniar aici,* "She has brought her load from the west". I recognised the allusion, because often, when turf was scarce, I had seen the women come down from the hills bent double under packs of heather. What a fine image, I thought, what eloquence! Before the day was out, I had heard the same expression from three or four different people. It was common property. After many similar experiences I realised that these gems falling from the lips of the people, so far from being novelties, were centuries old – they were what the language was made of; and as I became fluent in it they began to trip off my own tongue. Returning to Homer, I read him in a new light. He was a people's poet – aristocratic, no doubt, but living in an age in which class inequalities had not yet created a cultural cleavage between hut and castle. His language was artificial, yet, strange to say, this artificiality was natural. It was the language of the people raised to a higher power. . .

This Island influence is acknowledged in the first volume of his monumental *Studies in Ancient Greek Society, The Prehistoric Aegean,* which was published in 1949. It concentrated mainly on the Bronze Age and treated at length such fundamental topics as matriarchy, land-tenure, Aegean prehistory and the evolution of the epic. In the preface he proclaimed in forthright terms his attitude to Greek studies:

Everybody knows that for many years past their popularity has been declining, and the reason is that they have lost touch with the forces of human progress. Instead of being a message of hope for the future, as they were in the great days of humanism, they have become a pastime for a leisured minority striving ineffectually to find a refuge from it. Our Hellenic heritage must be rescued from the Mandarins, or else it will perish, destroyed by its devotees.

George Thomson would never be popular with the Mandarins!

The second volume of *Studies, The First Philosophers,* appeared in 1955 and concentrates on the growth of slavery and the ideas of the natural philosophers, forming a link between primitive thought and scientific knowledge. He discusses the relationship between ancient Greek and Chinese philosophy, a subject he pursued during a number of visits to China, including a period of six months in 1955 which he spent studying the language at the University of Peking. Some Chinese students also came to Birmingham to study Greek.

He paid his first visit to Russia in 1935, taking a particular interest in the progress of minority languages and cultures since the founding of the USSR. The socialist country with which he had the closest links was Czechoslovakia where he participated in annual conferences of classical scholars. He helped to develop the Marxist approach to classical and anthropological studies. One result was the establishment of *Eirene* (Peace), a cultural journal which still exists today. In 1960 he was elected to membership of the Czechoslovak Academy of Sciences and on his sixtieth birthday he was presented with *Geras,* published in Prague, studies by 24 classical scholars from Czechoslovakia, Bulgaria, Roumania, East Germany, Russia, Hungary, France, Britain and Ireland.

His books became known on every continent and were translated into 22 languages.

10

George Thomson's work was not of the study only; he was an active communist for many years, serving on various committees of the Party, including the national executive, for long periods. He was a member of the editorial board of *Modern Quarterly* and of its successor, *Marxism Today.* Both he and Katharine were active in the Party's cultural work.

He taught Marxist classes where he was noted for the clarity of his exposition of the subject, just as at Galway it was said he never had to fumble for the right word in Irish. This made him popular as a teacher in factory branches in Birmingham. On Sundays, with the men left at home, he taught the wives of factory workers about the role of women in society, long before the modern feminist movement arose. He gave talks on the English classics from Chaucer to Hardy. Of the latter, a particular favourite, he said: "As poet and novelist he spoke for the peasantry". He had always loved English literature, so much so that, after completing the first part of his Tripos at Cambridge, he would have switched to that subject if his tutors had not dissuaded him. And, into the last years of his life, he would continue to give classes in Marxism.

In the sixties, at the invitation of the Association of Greek Writers, he made four tours of Greece where he drew crowded audiences to hear him lecturing about Homer and the tragic poets, about the unbroken continuum of Hellenism through three thousand years. For one lecture, at the Rex Theatre in Athens, the police had to divert the traffic while crowds queued to get in! These tours were organised by his Greek son-in-law, Christos Alexiou, who also arranged for the lectures to be published in Greece. And, with the same genius as he had translated Greek into Irish, Irish into English, he was translating the modern Greek poets. In 1969 came his rendering, with a long introduction, of the *Twelve Lays of the Gipsy* by Kostís Palamás, "one of the greatest of all Greek poets".

For the China Policy Study Group he wrote a masterly introduction to Marxism in three books: *From Marx to Mao, a Study in Revolutionary Dialectics* (1972); *Capitalism and After, the Rise and Fall of Commodity Production* (1973); *The Human Essence, the Sources of Science and Art* (1974). His complete familiarity with the Marxist classics is shown by the extensive quotations from them. Indeed, in preparation he had read consecutively through the 45 volumes of the *Collected Works* of Lenin. He described the experience as like reading a giant Russian novel, except that Lenin was looking at the real world.

11

Music, of which he had a deep understanding, was important to George Thomson's life. It comes naturally to him in this last

book of his to say of *Twenty Years A-Growing,* "The story moves
like a piece of music".

Always there were the common origins of poetry and music
to pursue, since Greek poetry was wedded to music. The Blasket
experience had brought illumination when for the first time he
heard poems, known to him only on the printed page, sung by
traditional singers. The traditional Gaelic poet composes to
traditional airs, words wedded to music as in ancient Greece. A
poet like Carolan, whom Muiris O'Sullivan quotes, would com-
pose airs of his own.

In Birmingham Thomson followed closely the work of the Clarion Singers, a choir of Midland workers who brought their experience of factory and workshop into their interpretations of operatic
roles, giving them a new dimension. Katharine was an active
member of the choir as accompanist on the piano and as conduc-
tor. It was founded in 1940 by Dr Colin Bradsworth, who had
been a medical officer with the International Brigade in Spain.
Paul Robeson was its president for many years and the composer
Alan Bush now holds that office. Ralph Vaughan Williams was
a strong supporter and he came to hear them performing his *Sir
John in Love,* based on Shakespeare's *The Merry Wives of Windsor.*
He was ill at the time but was delighted by the performance and
returned home refreshed, saying, "Birmingham is the place to
recover in!"

Thomson always maintained that he learnt as much from discussions with the workers in his Marxist classes as they learnt
from him. In the same way he found it illuminating to listen to
the interpretations of the Clarion Singers. And, at home, discussions went on with Katharine about folk and classical music. He
believed that the great classical composers – Haydn, Mozart,
Beethoven, Schubert – had their roots in their native folk music.

Thomson had discussions with others too, among them
Kodály, the Hungarian composer who, like Bartok, and
Vaughan Williams in England, collected folk tunes and songs.
Kodály was a family friend who visited them in Cambridge and
also came to see them at Birmingham. Thomson gave him the
French translation of *Twenty Years A-Growing* and Kodály wrote
in September 1937:

> I finished here O'Sullivan's book with great pleasure, the
> more since a quite similar book exists in Hungarian. Not

written by the peasant himself, but nearly so: he told his life to one of our best writers who stenographed the talk, and hardly added anything but a little ordered the whole.

The "20 ans" is charming, although the French is, I suppose, quite unable to render the style of the original. It should be translated into Hungarian and I will try to interest some publisher.

Please give my best regards to Stewarts and your wife.

Yours cordially,

Z Kodály

PS Be so kind if you find time to write out for me the passage about dirge in English and Irish. P. 106 "Quatre hommes. . . les vis rire joyeusement entre elles."

The passage referred to here is from the chapter "The Wake":

Four men brought out the coffin and rested it on two chairs. The old women gathering round it began to moan, sweet and soft: "Olagón, olagón!"

It was for Kate Joseph's voice I listened, for she was reputed to be like a banshee for keening.

"Oh, musha, Kate," she began with a fine tune on the words, "isn't it you were the graceful woman, and it is little profit for me to live after you, olagón! olagón! olagón!"

When they had finished their keening I saw them laughing merrily with one another.

Katharine has recorded ex-Blasket fiddlers in West Kerry: Tom Daly, noted for his rendering of "Port na bPúcaí", fairy music first heard on Inish Vickillaun, and Seán Mhicil O'Sullivan, the last man to leave the Island.

How closely Katharine and George worked together can be seen from her book *The Masonic Thread in Mozart*, published in 1977, and his book *The Human Essence* with its sections on "The Symphony and the Novel", "Symphonic Form" and "Beethoven". In this last section he compares Aeschylus with the composer:

Aeschylus and Beethoven both possessed a profound sense of dialectics, which enabled them to reveal in the form and content of their work the contradictions underlying the social movement of their time. Hence, if their work has a permanent value as a source of inspiration for subsequent generations, that is not because it embodies absolute truths, valid for all ages, but because in their own lifetime it was so intensely contemporary.

If this criterion is accepted, it must be granted that Beethoven was the greater artist.

12

In 1970 George Thomson retired from the Chair of Greek at Birmingham. One of the first tasks he now undertook was to prepare a second edition of the Irish text of *Twenty Years A-Growing* which had been out of print since 1941. He had always kept the manuscript, along with drawings Muiris O'Sullivan made to illustrate it. The old text was in Gaelic script and in the accepted spelling of the time. The new text is in Roman and conforms to the spelling now standard, while retaining the flavour of the West Kerry dialect; this latter a very important point with Thomson. It was a slow task because he was suffering from failing eyesight but, as he writes in the preface, "I undertook this work out of love for the people of the Island and especially for the dearest of all my friends".

The question arose once again of finding a suitable publisher. The professor of Modern Irish at St Patrick's College, Maynooth, Fr Pádraig Ó Fiannachta from West Kerry, had already collaborated with Thomson in producing *Mise Agaistín* (The Confessions of St Augustine) in 1967. When he left Galway Thomson had translated the first four books, and a quarter of a century later Fr Ó Fiannachta translated six more. The book was published by An Sagart of Maynooth. It made a profit, but Thomson would not accept any of this, suggesting instead that it be put into the funds of An Sagart. "In this way," says Fr Ó Fiannachta, "he was the first person to lay the foundations of the fund which published so cheaply the *Lectionary*, the *Book of the Roman Mass* and the *Holy Bible* in Irish."

Fr Ó Fiannachta now stepped forward when he heard that Thomson was looking for a publisher who would accept his views about editing. He came over to Birmingham and spent a week with Thomson checking the typescript and consulting the manuscript where necessary. About that week he wrote a poem in Irish which appeared in a collection of his Irish lyrics, *Donn Bó*:

> In Partnership over *Fiche Blian*
> To George, in Birmingham, 19/10/75
>
> The Great Blasket
> The Inish, the Feo,
> Sheep, rabbits and puffins
> Did not bind our partnership. No,
> But Muiris, Mícheál, old Owen,
> Women, girls and young folk,
> Alive on each page,
> The dead who were dead
> Called back to the stage.

The second edition of *Fiche Blian ag Fás* appeared in 1976, with acknowledgements to Fr Ó Fiannachta. It was launched at the Listowel Writers' Week. George and Katharine came over for the event at which he spoke in Irish as fluently as ever. They went on to West Kerry where Proinsias Mac Aonghusa interviewed him in Irish for Radió Éireann. He called on his old friend Mícheál O'Guiheen, known as "The Poet", who was now living at Dunquin. "He was overjoyed, and we spent an hour together casting our minds back to the days of our youth, which he recalled as vividly as if it had all happened only the week before." So Thomson wrote in the foreword he supplied for *A Pity Youth Does Not Last,* a translation of Mícheál's *Is Truagh Ná Fanann an Óige* which Oxford University Press published, along with some of his poems, in 1982.

About this visit to Kerry Thomson wrote to Fr Ó Fiannachta: "I felt rather like Oisín might have done if he had received from St Patrick a special dispensation to revisit the Land of the Young".

He went through the text again for a third edition. He was having to use a magnifier but this had the compensating advantage, he said, of enabling him to discover any errors and discrepancies still remaining. This work he eventually completed. The book, "fresh and savoury as new risen bread", as an earlier critic had said of it, has become a popular favourite with a new generation of Gaelic readers.

In 1977 An Sagart published *An Blascaod a Bhí,* an essay on the Blasket writers and their cultural background in which Thomson, still writing easily in Irish, said:

> We have a small library the like of which is not to be found in any other language. They are books apart which have won a corner for themselves in international literature.

In 1982 An Sagart published an expanded English version, *The Blasket that was.*

13

He had links with the University of Thessaloniki, where students from Birmingham spent a year as part of their course, and in 1979 the University conferred an honorary degree on him. For that occasion he wrote *The Problem of the Bacchae,* in which the play of Euripedes is discussed in relation to drug addiction today. This lecture, prepared with the co-operation of Dr Bernard Barnett, was read for him by Christos Alexiou since he was unable to attend owing to ill-health. It was published as a monograph at Thessaloniki.

"The Inter-University Committee on the Modern Greek Language in the Universities of the English-speaking World" presented a Certificate of Achievement to him in 1980 "in recognition of the resolute support of and extraordinary contribution to the development of the discipline of Modern Greek". From Thessaloniki in 1984 came another monograph, *Language and Labour,* an attempt "to show how Marx's analysis of the labour-process can be used to throw light on the origin of grammatical categories". It was an extension of an argument he had already put forward in *The First Philosophers* and *The Human Essence.* In one section of the work he quotes Greek, Chinese, Russian, German, French and Irish versions of well-known English proverbs. This extraordinary man was then 81! He had for long been an honorary member of the Association of Greek Writers and in the year before he died he was made a free citizen of Eleusis, birthplace of Aeschylus.

Ireland too had never forgotten George Thomson. With the revival of interest in the Blasket in recent years, his home became a Mecca for those seeking Blasket lore. He was only too willing to share his unrivalled knowledge with them, as I have good reason to know. He was *Oisín i ndiaidh na Féinne,* "Oisín left alone now that the Fianna were all gone". In a letter to Walter McGrath who, as a young reporter for the *Cork Examiner,* had witnessed the evacuation of the Island in 1953, he said that he had never expected to be making new friendships in his old age. One of these was with the West Kerry Gaelic scholar, historian and poet Seán Ó Lúing, who gave a memorable address in Irish on his life and work to the Kerry Archaeological and Historical Society in 1980.[4]

From 9 January 1981 to 16 February 1981 a series of well researched articles about him by the West Cork teacher, journalist and Gaelic writer, Risteárd Ó Glaisne, appeared in the Gaelic weekly *Inniu*. From 17 April to 1 June three more articles appeared there written by Máirtín O'Flaherty, formerly secretary to President de Valera, about Thomson's period at Galway, where O'Flaherty had been a student at the time and had attended Thomson's Greek lectures.

In an interview with Pádraig Tyers, quoted in *Leoithne Aniar,* Seán O'Crohan, son of Tomás, said:

> George had better Irish than Muiris himself, indeed than all the rest of us. He did wonderful work on Muiris's book, both in Irish and in English. George was in every sense a gentleman because of all he did for the people of the Island and the help he gave them.

A book in Irish by Nuala Ní Aimhirgín about Muiris O'Sullivan appeared in 1983 and in it Thomson figures prominently.[5] That was the year of his eightieth birthday which was celebrated in Ireland and amongst the ex-Islanders in Massachusetts. A tribute in the *Cork Evening Echo* ended: "From Ireland which owes him so much we salute him". Holiday visitors to the Blasket

celebrated with readings from *Twenty Years A-Growing*.
J. Nevill Birdsall, Professor of Theology, wrote in the *Birmingham University Weekly* of their Emeritus Professor of Greek:

> Although we must be sorry to hear that his health has
> deteriorated with advancing years, we can congratulate him
> on attaining this age, and on the continued and unhampered
> vigour of his mind. A few years ago, a Franciscan of the
> Galway priory gave a message to transmit from his elder
> brethren who had learnt their Greek from George Thomson.
> "Tell Seoirse Mac Tomáis that the Franciscans of Galway
> have not forgotten him"; on another occasion, a professor
> of Celtic from an American university, coming here after a
> visit to Ireland, told me that the name of Seoirse Mac
> Tomáis was often on the lips of men in the West. In 1963
> I took on the teaching of elementary Greek in my depart-
> ment: and until 1971 as a teacher followed George Thom-
> son's guidance. The practice of the method as a teacher is
> one of the most testing disciplines to which I have ever been
> subjected: and one of the most rewarding. I know that many
> of my pupils found it so – although it must be admitted that
> to benefit from it, one must long to master Greek before
> engaging on this testing course. It also revitalised my study
> of other languages: and brought, by analogy, new insights
> to the study of exegesis and the thought of the "biblical
> world".
>
> He was also, and is, a friend. I am sure that not only I
> can say that his encouragement was one of the pillars upon
> which my teaching and research have rested. He remains
> an example to us all who knew him of true scholarship and
> of the ideal of university teaching.

In 1985 he appeared in the outstanding documentary film on
the literary and cultural legacy of the Blasket, *Oileán Eile*, written
and directed for Radió Telefís Éireann by Muiris Mac Conghail.
A film crew had visited his home for the purpose and his contribu-
tion was widely acclaimed, not least by ex-Islanders. In
Springfield, Massachusetts, Professor Tom Biuso, who has for
some years been collecting Blasket lore in America, brought ex-
Islanders together in the home of Mrs Eileen Calullane (Eibhlín
Pats Tom Kearney) to watch a video of it. She wrote to tell
Thomson how much they enjoyed it and, of course, there were

"a lot of tears shed too". He had spoken so well "about the Blaskets and the people there that anybody will be proud to be a Blasket Islander".

In 1986 Seán Ó Lúing and his son Gearóid came over to Birmingham to be presented on behalf of the National Library of Ireland with Muiris O'Sullivan's manuscript of *Twenty Years A-Growing* – Thomson's most treasured possession. And all the time he was working indomitably on with the aid of a magnifier and a small microphone to sustain conversation, as his voice had become enfeebled. He was re-writing and expanding his book on the Blasket and had to have pages of the first draft blown up into larger print to help with his work.

14

I myself paid what would be the last of many visits down the years to him, just before Christmas. He was ill in bed but insisted on getting up and being helped to a chair in his bedroom. *Bean an Oileáin* by Máire Guiheen had recently been published with acknowledgements to Joan Stagles and Professor George Thomson "for their encouragement and help". Joan, with her husband Ray Stagles, had written *The Blasket Islands*. I read a passage to him where Máire tells of other children calling to her house in the morning to con their lessons before they all set off for school:

> I remember one morning when we were all there, learning some poem, and my mother kept saying "Ye're making too much noise". George Thomson was in the room at the end of the house asleep. "Ye'll wake up George, so keep the voices down."

George Thomson had a phenomenal memory. He could not only recall listening with delight to the children but even the poem they were learning – *The Brook* by Tennyson. On a visit not long before the name of Mícheál Ó Guiheen had cropped up and suddenly he recalled a quatrain Mícheál made about the bad weather back in 1924:

> Blian gan teas gan tine,
> Blian gan bia le n-ithe,
> Blian gan iasc sna sruthaibh,
> Ná ceol na n-éan ba bhinne.

> A year without fire or heat,
> A year without food to eat,
> A year without fish in the streams,
> Or songs of the birds so sweet.

It will be no surprise to say that he would talk learnedly about the culture of the Blasket with cross-references to many different cultures, ancient and modern. It may cause surprise that he could also unravel as well as any Islander the complicated family relationships, not only within the Blasket but with people on the nearby mainland.

Over the Christmas his daughter Margaret was home on holiday from Harvard, and she helped him with the revision of the book. It was to her that he dictated "The Sorrowful Cliff" section of *Twenty Years A-Growing*.

Towards the end of January he had to postpone a visit from Ray Stagles and put off another visitor who was gathering materials for a biography of Ludwig Wittgenstein, the Logical Positivist. Thomson had written "Some Personal Recollections" of Wittgenstein for *Revolutionary World*, an international philosophy journal, in 1980. Though they held diametrically opposite philosophical positions, the two men were good friends, drawn together, Thomson thought, "by a common distaste for the intellectual life of Cambridge. He was very musical. He used to come to our house on Thursdays and spend the evening with Katharine going through Schubert's *Lieder*."

Thomson did manage to finish his book. On 3 February, the very morning of the day he died, I received a letter from Katharine listing, with captions, the photographs she and George had selected as illustrations, some of them taken during his first visit to the Blasket in 1923. One was of himself though, typically, Katharine had to persuade him to allow this to go in.

Typical too is the title of the last chapter of his book, "The Blasket that will be", and its closing lines which show that his faith in the ultimate triumph of "the deprived and the dispossessed" across the world remained undimmed. In 1976 he had sent a Christmas card to Fr Ó Fiannachta illustrated with a picture of the people of a village commune in China drawing in a net full of fish from a small lake. On the card he had written: "See how my vision of the Blasket is being realised in China today". Was he planning any further work? The answer is yes.[6] About Eoghan Rua O'Sullivan Fr Pádraig Dinneen had said in his edition of that poet, "What Pindar is to Greece Eoghan Rua is to Ireland". He agreed with this, adding that a useful monograph might be written comparing – I need hardly add favourably – the poets of the *aisling*, the eighteenth century "vision" poets like Aogán O'Rahilly and Eoghan Rua O'Sullivan, with Pindar, the greatest lyric poet of ancient Greece. And I need hardly add also that no one could have written on that subject with more illumination than George Derwent Thomson.

Since this memoir of George Thomson's many-sided life and work began with Máire Guiheen's description of his arrival on the Great Blasket Island in 1923, let Máire have the last word about him:

Bhí sé uasal íseal.
He was a noble person, he loved the people.

Tim Enright
March, 1988

Notes

Before the Famine
1. *Scéalta ón mBlascaod, p.40*
2. *Seanchas ón Oileán Tiar*, p. 262

The Land
1. *Leoithne Aniar*, pp. 16-17

Improvised Verse
1. *Seanchas ón Oileán Tiar*, p. 40

The Mythical Background
1. *Seanchas ón Oileán Tiar*, p. 207

Fuit Ilium
1. *Lá Dár Saol*, p. 4

Buying and Selling
1. *Leoithne Aniar*, pp. 70-71

Memoir
1. I am most grateful to Máire Guiheen for sending me an account of George Thomson on the Island. Besides *Bean an Oileáin*, which is mentioned in the memoir, Máire, who now lives in Clogher, wrote *An tOileán a Bhí*, "The Island That Was".
2. *Odyssey IX*, l. 27
3. *Hermathena*, May 1939
4. *Journal of the Kerry Archaeological Society*, No 13, 1980. This is the third of Seán Ó Lúing's scholarly and invaluable studies of famous scholars who sojourned on the Blasket. The others were of Robin Flower and of Carl Marstrander the Norwegian Celtic scholar who had advised Flower to go to the Island. With his usual ready generosity Seán Ó Lúing has also sent me additional information. He has now compiled and edited for publication as a volume the Gaelic articles and stories George Thomson wrote for journals and newspapers during the years 1926-1934 when he was active in the Gaelic revival.
5. The first book about a Blasket writer and welcome not only for the interest of the subject but for the information it contains about the Island. Both Nuala Ní Aimhirgín and Seán Ó Lúing quote from the

151

Irish diaries of Eibhlín O'Sullivan and Mícheál O'Guiheen which have not been published; they are in the National Library.
6. Translations of Homer's *Iliad Book I*, the *Symposium* of Plato and *Idyll XV* of Theocritus were found after George Thomson's death. Fr Pádraig Ó Fiannachta has edited them and has published *Iliad I* and *Idyll XV* in *Léachtaí Cholm Cille XVIII* (1988) and the first half of the *Symposium* in *Irisleabhar Mhá Nuad* (1988). He hopes to publish the second half in *Irisleabhar* 1989.

Bibliography

Delargy, J. A. "The Gaelic Storyteller", *Proceedings of the British Academy*, Vol xxx, 1945

Flower, R. *The Western Island*, Oxford 1944, 1978

Greene, D. and O'Connor, F. *Golden Treasury of Irish Verse*, London 1967

Hardy, F. E. *Life of Thomas Hardy*, London 1967

Hardy, T. *Collected Poems*, London 1933

Í Cearnaigh, S. *An tOileán a Tréigeadh*, Dublin 1974

— *Iarbhlascaodach ina Dheoraí*, Dublin 1978

Jackson, K. *Early Celtic Nature Poetry*, Cambridge 1935

Luce, J. V. *Homeric Qualities in the Life and Literature of the Great Blasket Island, Greece and Rome* Vol xvi, 1969

Meyer, K. *Selections from Ancient Irish Poetry*, London 1911

Ní Aimhirgín, N. *Muiris Ó Súilleabháin*, Maynooth 1983

Ní Ghuithín, M. *An tOileán a Bhí*, Dublin 1978

— *Bean an Oileáin*, Dublin 1986

Ní Shúilleabháin, E. *Letters from the Great Blasket*, Cork 1978

Ó Criomhthain, S. *Lá Dár Saol*, Dublin 1969

— *Leoithne Aniar*, Ballyferriter 1982

Ó Criomhthain, T. *Réiltíní Óir*, 2 vol, ed. Fr Seoirse MacClúin, Dublin 1922

— *Allagar na hInise*, Dublin 1928, 1977

— *Island Cross-Talk*, Oxford 1986

— *An tOileánach*, Dublin 1929, 1973

— *The Islandman*, London 1937, Oxford 1951

— *Dinnsheanchas na mBlascaodaí*, Dublin 1928

— *Seanchas ón Oileán Tiar*, Dublin 1956

Ó Gaoithín, M. *Is Truagh ná Fanann an Óige*, Dublin 1953

— *A Pity Youth Does Not Last*, Oxford 1982

— *Coinnle Corra*, Dublin 1968

— *Beatha Pheig Sayers*, Dublin 1970

O'Rahilly, T. F. *Measgra Dánta*, Cork 1927

Ó Súilleabháin, M. *Fiche Blian ag Fás*, Dublin 1933, Maynooth 1976

— *Twenty Years A-Growing*, London 1933, Oxford 1953

O'Sullivan, D. *Songs of the Irish*, Dublin 1960

Ó Tuama, S. and Kinsella, T. *An Duanaire*, Dublin 1981

Sayers, P. *Peig*, Dublin 1936

— *Peig, the autobiography of Peig Sayers*, Dublin 1974

— *Machnamh Seanmhná*, Dublin 1939

— *An Old Woman's Reflections,* Oxford 1962
— *Scéalta ón mBlascoad,* Dublin 1938
Stagles, J. and R. *The Blasket Islands,* Dublin 1980
Synge, J. M. *The Aran Islands,* Dublin 1906
Yeats, W. B. *Collected Poems,* London 1933